Annotated Legal Documents on Islam in Europe: European Court of Human Rights

Annotated Legal Documents on Islam in Europe

VOLUME 26

The titles published in this series are listed at *brill.com/ldie*

Annotated Legal Documents on Islam in Europe

European Court of Human Rights

Compiled, Annotated and Authored by

Fedor Arkhipov

BRILL

LEIDEN | BOSTON

The Library of Congress Cataloging-in-Publication Data is available online at https://catalog.loc.gov

Typeface for the Latin, Greek, and Cyrillic scripts: "Brill". See and download: brill.com/brill-typeface.

ISSN 2214-1340
ISBN 978-90-04-74555-1 (paperback)

This book is printed on acid-free paper and produced in a sustainable manner.

Contents

Foreword by the Editors

This is the 26th volume in the series *Annotated Legal Documents on Islam in Europe*. The publication of this series responds to the widespread lack of sound information about the legal status of Islam in Europe. In principle, this information is easily available to those who are willing to make the effort and know enough about the subject to ask the right questions of the digital search engines. But that requires both expertise and effort, and it takes place in an environment in which the public political debate on Islam in many European countries is characterised by increasing concern and fear. Islam has come to be perceived broadly as a security issue rather than a religion like others in Europe. But the concern has also moved into the legal field, most markedly, of course, with discussions about limitations on Muslim female dress enacted in a growing number of countries, or the ban on building minarets or mosques in Switzerland, or restrictions on building mosques in certain Austrian provinces. At the same time, in a number of European states like Austria and Germany, legislation is enacted and state treaties are negotiated which aim to establish a stable and reliable basis for Muslim life and organisation. Even so, such measures are under scrutiny from an increasingly sceptical European public, which sometimes ignores the legal principles of secularity, not least the demands of state neutrality towards and the equal treatment of all religions and beliefs regardless of the numbers of their adherents or their public reputation.

In addition, the religious status and rights of Muslims in the various European countries differ significantly, due to different historical developments regarding the organisation of relations between the state and religions. Furthermore, while in some states laws regulating such matters introduced decades ago are still in force and have to be re-interpreted in the face of a 'newcomer' religion, others have introduced new laws that consider the increasing religious plurality within Europe. Despite the common legal and political foundations constructed since 1945 in instruments such as the European Convention on Human Rights and the more recently accumulated legislation of the European Union, this closer look reveals remarkable differences due to the extent of separating state and religion or establishing co-operative structures. In some countries Islam has an officially recognised status which in some cases originated in the first half of the 20th century. In other countries no such recognition of any religion is available, even if informal ways of favouring one religion over another may exist. Since 1990 especially, European courts have moved to equalise the status of Islam with that of other religions in the practical exercise of religious freedom in various countries. Particular practices regarded as core religious obligations—in the case of Muslims dress codes and practices such as male circumcision, access to correctly slaughtered meat and otherwise *halal* food, free time for the main periods of worship and religious festivals, and the right to build mosques—can be controversial in some countries while less so in others. In the course of the ongoing process of self-organisation and the participation of Muslims in civil societies and their co-operation with the state, children's access to Islamic religious instruction or the education of Muslim theologians can be achieved in co-operation with the state education systems in some countries, while in others the community must rely on its own arrangements. The practically pressing issue of financing the religious infrastructure is still far from being settled in many countries.

The aim of this series is to make this legislation available to both the interested researcher and the practising lawyer. Altogether the series is expected to comprise 32 volumes, one for each of the 27 countries of the European Union plus Norway, Switzerland and the United Kingdom, and volumes each dealing with the European Union (treaties, directives and decisions of the Court of Justice of the European Communities) and the European Court of Human Rights. Excerpts from relevant legislation are introduced and summarised by the volume compiler/author, and where court cases have provided significant interpretation of the law they will also be referred to. The legislation itself is reproduced in the original language, as the editors and the publisher agreed early on in the preparation of the series that any attempt to translate legislation into English would be unsatisfactory and risked being misleading. The comments and analysis by the author should give sufficient guidance to users to allow for a decision whether to arrange a translation for their specific purposes.

The European Court of Human Rights, based in Strasbourg, France, was established in 1950 by the European Convention for the Protection of Human Rights and Fundamental Freedoms to 'ensure the observance' of the Convention, commonly called the European Convention of Human Rights (ECHR). Since its initial adoption a number of subsequent protocols has developed the Convention further.[1] The Convention is binding on member states of the Council of Europe, and the Court is made up of judges appointed by the member states, one from each member.

An attempt has been made to ensure that the volumes are structured in as similar a manner as possible. The starting point for this has been the them-

1 Bates, ed. *The evolution of the European Convention on Human Rights: from its inception to the creation of a permanent Court of Human Rights*. (Oxford: Oxford University Press, 2010).

atic organisation used variously in the *Yearbook of Muslims in Europe* which Brill has published annually since 2009. In the case of the present volume it has been only a starting point, and the compiler and the editors have agreed on the structure which makes most sense for the ECtHR. Normally one member of the editorial group takes responsibility for discussing the structure and compilation of each volume with the compiler: in this instance, this task was undertaken by Professor Silvio Ferrari. We are also grateful to Kate Elliott for the care shown in copy editing the volume. The initiative for this project came from the publisher, where Nicolette van der Hoek and Nienke Brienen-Moolenaar have played an invaluable role in ensuring that the project has maintained its momentum. As editors, we appreciate how much their expertise contributes to ensuring that a project like this can run smoothly.

The Editors, April 2025

General Introduction

Islam has a significant presence in Europe, in countries both with predominantly Muslim populations and those in which Muslims constitute a minority. This diversity underscores the complex interaction between Islamic beliefs and European legal frameworks, particularly within the context of the European Convention on Human Rights. This book offers a comprehensive review of the ECtHR's practice in cases related to violations of the religious freedoms of Muslims, shedding light on the legal dynamics, challenges and trends in this area.

The situation of Islam in countries party to the European Convention varies widely, reflecting diverse historical, cultural and political contexts. In nations with overwhelmingly Islamic populations, such as Turkey, the relationship between Islamic law (Sharia) and secular legal systems has been a subject of debate and contention.[1] The coexistence of Islamic principles with modern legal frameworks poses challenges, as interpretations of Sharia may conflict with European legal norms, particularly regarding issues such as family law, women's rights and religious freedom.[2]

Contradictions between European and Islamic law further complicate the landscape. While European legal systems prioritise secularism, individual rights and equality, Islamic law encompasses religious precepts, social norms and cultural practices rooted in Islamic tradition. The principle of secularism in European law is based on the separation of religious and state institutions, ensuring that the government remains neutral regarding religious matters, and guarantees freedom of belief to all citizens. However, it is important to note that not all European countries prioritise secularism equally.[3] For example, the United Kingdom has an established Anglican Church for England, and in countries like Greece, where the Orthodox Christian faith is predominant, religious traditions are closely intertwined with state institutions. Thus, while secularism is widely supported across Europe, its application varies based on the historical and cultural context of each nation. Nevertheless, the concept of Sharia, which governs various aspects of Muslim life, including family law, inheritance

1 Emon, Anver M., *Religious pluralism and Islamic law: Dhimmis and others in the Empire of Law* (Oxford: Oxford University Press, 2012), p. 105.

2 Cavalcanti, Maria, 'Islamic family law and legal pluralism approach: Case studies of reasonable accommodation in Europe', *Ius Comparatum* 2022.2, pp. 352–388.

3 Moniz, Jorge Botelho, 'Secularization in Europe: Causes, Consequences, and Cultural Diversity', *Religions* 14.3 (2023), p. 423.

and personal conduct, may diverge from European legal principles, leading to tensions and legal disputes.[4]

The political dimension of the problem underlines its complexity. Debates surrounding the accommodation of Islamic practices within European societies often intersect with broader discussions on multiculturalism, secularism and national identity.[5] The rise of Islamophobia, fuelled by societal prejudices and political rhetoric, further exacerbates the challenges faced by Muslim communities in Europe.[6] Against this backdrop, the ECtHR serves as a crucial arbiter, balancing individual rights with state interests and upholding the principles of the European Convention.

This review focuses exclusively on the legal aspects of violations of the religious freedoms of Muslims, aiming to provide a nuanced understanding of the ECtHR's jurisprudence in this areaWhile acknowledging the multifaceted nature of the issue, the review adopts a legal lens to analyse key cases, principles and trends, offering insights into the evolving landscape of religious freedoms in Europe. The process from application to decision in the European Court of Human Rights typically begins with the submission of an application by an individual or a group claiming a violation of its rights under the European Convention on Human Rights.[7] The Court examines the admissibility of the case, which involves determining whether it falls within its jurisdiction and whether domestic remedies have been exhausted. If the application is deemed admissible, the Court proceeds to a detailed examination of the facts, legal arguments and relevant case law. The case may be heard by a panel of judges and, following deliberation, a judgment is issued which can include findings of a violation, compensation or other forms of redress for the applicants. Decisions made by the Court are binding on the state involved, although the parties may appeal to the Grand Chamber for a final ruling in particularly significant or complex cases.

The book is structured into 12 sections, each dedicated to a main group of ECtHR cases involving Muslims. Within each section, thematic parts further

---

4 An-Naim, Abdullahi Ahmed, *Islam and the secular state: Negotiating the future of Sharia.* (Cambridge, MA: Harvard University Press, 2008), pp. 30–31.

5 For example see Sofos, Spyros A., and Tsagarousianou, Roza, *Islam in Europe: Public Spaces and Civic Networks.* (London: Palgrave Macmillan, 2013).

6 Helbling, Marc, and Traunmüller, Richard, 'What is Islamophobia? Disentangling citizens' feelings toward ethnicity, religion and religiosity using a survey experiment', *British Journal of Political Science* 50.3 (2020): 811–828.

7 European Court of Human Rights. *Your application to the ECHR: How to apply and how your application is processed.* Council of Europe, Strasbourg, France. www.echr.coe.int/documents/d/echr/your_application_eng.

explore specific aspects of the cases, providing detailed analysis and commentary. This structure allows for a comprehensive examination of the legal complexities and trends within each thematic area. Each section delves into specific legal issues, offering insights into the ECtHR's approach, key precedents and emerging trends. Following the thematic parts, brief analyses provide additional commentary and context, enhancing understanding of the complex legal dynamics at play.

The role of the European Court of Human Rights in shaping perceptions and attitudes towards Islam extends beyond its direct impact on legal outcomes.[8] While the Court's judgments have tangible effects on legal systems and individual rights claims, they also convey broader messages about Islam, law and Europeanisation. Through its decisions, the ECtHR communicates nuanced interpretations of relevant articles of the European Convention on Human Rights, shaping societal discourse and perceptions of religious freedoms.

---

8 Fokas, Effie, 'Islam at the European Court of Human Rights', *NAVEIÑ REET: Nordic Journal of Law and Social Research* 2021, 10 pp. 121–144.

CHAPTER 1

Relevant Articles of the Convention

A key aspect of the ECtHR's role is its interpretation of Articles within the ECHR that pertain to religious freedoms. Article 9, which safeguards the freedom of religion or belief, is central to many cases involving Islam. This Article protects the freedoms of thought, conscience and religion, emphasising their significance in a democratic society. However, it also allows for limitations on the manifestation of religion or belief, provided that they are prescribed by law and necessary in a democratic society. The ECtHR's landmark judgment in *Kokkinakis v. Greece* (1993) established a precedent emphasising the importance of religious freedom as a cornerstone of democracy, reflecting the pluralism essential to democratic societies.[1]

Article 9 of the European Convention on Human Rights—Freedom of thought, conscience and religion

1. Everyone has the right to freedom of thought, conscience and religion; this right includes freedom to change her/his religion or belief and freedom, either alone or in community with others and in public or private, to manifest her/his religion or belief, in worship, teaching, practice and observance.
2. Freedom to manifest one's religion or beliefs shall be subject only to such limitations as are prescribed by law and are necessary in a democratic society in the interests of public safety, for the protection of public order, health or morals, or for the protection of the rights and freedoms of others.

In addition to Article 9, other Articles frequently invoked in cases involving Islam include Articles 10, 11 and 14, and Article 2 of the 1st Protocol to the Convention. Article 10 protects the freedom of expression, including the right to hold opinions and receive and impart information. Like those relating to the freedom of religion, this right is subject to limitations in the interests of national security, public safety and the protection of others' rights. Article 11

1 Kokkinakis v Greece—14307/88, A/260-A, [1993] ECHR 20, (1994) 17 EHRR 397, IHRL 2980 (ECHR 1993) (25 May 1993).

guarantees the freedom of assembly and association, with similar restrictions intended to protect public order and safety.

Article 10 Freedom of expression

1. Everyone has the right to freedom of expression. This right shall include freedom to hold opinions and to receive and impart information and ideas without interference by public authority and regardless of frontiers. This article shall not prevent States from requiring the licensing of broadcasting, television or cinema enterprises.
2. The exercise of these freedoms, since it carries with it duties and responsibilities, may be subject to such formalities, conditions, restrictions or penalties as are prescribed by law and are necessary in a democratic society, in the interests of national security, territorial integrity or public safety, for the prevention of disorder or crime, for the protection of health or morals, for the protection of the reputation or rights of others, for preventing the disclosure of information received in confidence, or for maintaining the authority and impartiality of the judiciary.

Article 11 Freedom of assembly and association

1. Everyone has the right to freedom of peaceful assembly and to freedom of association with others, including the right to form and to join trade unions for the protection of his interests.
2. No restrictions shall be placed on the exercise of these rights other than such as are prescribed by law and are necessary in a democratic society in the interests of national security or public safety, for the prevention of disorder or crime, for the protection of health or morals or for the protection of the rights and freedoms of others. This article shall not prevent the imposition of lawful restrictions on the exercise of these rights by members of the armed forces, of the police or of the administration of the State.

Article 14 prohibits discrimination on various grounds, including religion, highlighting the ECtHR's commitment to combating discrimination against Muslims. Finally, Article 2 of the 1st Protocol ensures the right to education in conformity with one's religious and philosophical convictions. These Articles provide a framework for the ECtHR's analysis of cases involving Islam, addressing issues such as religious expression, discrimination and education.

Article 14 Prohibition of Discrimination

The enjoyment of the rights and freedoms set forth in this Convention shall be secured without discrimination on any ground such as sex, race, colour, language, religion, political or other opinion, national or social origin, association with a national minority, property, birth or other status.

....

Article 2 of Protocol 1 Right to education

No person shall be denied the right to education. In the exercise of any functions which it assumes in relation to education and to teaching, the State shall respect the right of parents to ensure such education and teaching in conformity with their own religions and philosophical convictions

It is especially necessary to discuss the provisions of Article 14 ECHR, as it plays a key role in protecting against discrimination in the exercise of rights guaranteed by the Convention. This Article prohibits discrimination on various grounds, such as gender, race, religion, national origin and others, and serves as a legal foundation for protecting individuals from discriminatory practices in different areas of life. In the context of reviewing the case law of the European Court of Human Rights regarding discrimination and violations of the religious freedom of Muslims, it is important that the Court's further interpretation be made with due regard to the provisions of Article 14.

Article 14 does not itself guarantee the right to equality, but it is an important tool in cases where discrimination hinders the enjoyment of other rights protected by the Convention. Therefore, when analysing cases related to discrimination on the grounds of religion, it should be noted that Article 14 is applied not independently but in conjunction with other rights, such as the right to freedom of religion or that to respect for private life.[2] This means that claims of discrimination should be considered in contexts in which religious rights are hindered or violated due to differential treatment.

Additionally, Article 14 includes an open list of grounds for discrimination, among which religion occupies a special place. The Court has repeatedly

2 Mjöll Arnardóttir, Oddný, 'Vulnerability under Article 14 of the European Convention on Human Rights: Innovation or Business as Usual?', *Oslo Law Review* 4.3 (2017), pp. 150–171.

emphasised the importance of freedom of religion and has established strict requirements for justifying differences in treatment based on religious affiliation. For example, in the *Vojnity v. Hungary* case (2013), the Court stated that to justify distinctions based on religion, 'weighty reasons' must be provided.[3] In matters concerning the rights of Muslims in Europe this requirement becomes particularly relevant, as religious practices often become the subject of discrimination or restrictions, especially in relation to practices such as wearing religious clothing or symbols.

At the same time, the open list of grounds for discrimination provided in Article 14 allows for the consideration of new forms of discrimination that may arise in a changing society. In particular, the European Court of Human Rights does not limit itself to the grounds explicitly mentioned in the Article but allows for the inclusion of other grounds, such as sexual orientation, disability or migrant status. This open formulation enables a flexible interpretation of the Article, which is especially important in cases related to religious discrimination.

An important element of the Court's approach is also its equating of violence motivated by religious hatred with violence based on racial hatred. In the *Milanovic v. Serbia* case (2010), the Court noted that violence with a religious undertone has a particularly destructive effect on human rights, which underscores the importance of protecting religious minorities.[4] These approaches allow us clearly to understand how the European Court balances the interests of public security and order with the rights of individuals, including Muslims, who face religious discrimination.

Thus, in this review of ECtHR cases related to discrimination and violations of the religious freedom of Muslims it is essential to consider the provisions of Article 14, as it provides an important legal context for assessing the justification of differential treatment on religious grounds. All further interpretations and analyses of case law should be based on the understanding of how Article 14 ECHR ensures protection against discrimination and how it relates to other rights guaranteed by the Convention.

The ECtHR's judgments reflect a delicate balance between safeguarding individual rights and respecting State interests. While the Court upholds the principles of religious freedom and non-discrimination, it also recognises the need for limitations in certain circumstances. The concepts of 'necessary in a democratic society' and 'public order' often feature prominently in the Court's

3 Vojnity v. Hungary—29617/07—Legal Summary [2013] ECHR 426 (12 February 2013).
4 Milanovic v. Serbia—44614/07 [2010] ECHR 2029 (14 December 2010).

decisions, illustrating the complex legal terrain surrounding religious freedoms.

Overall, the ECtHR's practice in cases related to violations of the religious freedoms of Muslims serves as a lens through which to understand broader issues of law, religion and societal norms. By examining the Court's interpretations of key articles of the ECtHR, scholars and policymakers gain insights into the evolving landscape of religious freedoms in Europe and the complex interplay between legal principles, cultural values and political realities.

CHAPTER 2

ECtHR Criteria for Determining Violation of Religious Freedoms in Cases Involving Muslims

There exists a fundamental divergence in the status of religion between the Muslim world and the secular West. In numerous European countries any extension of Islam beyond its religious confines is perceived as an intrusion upon the secular foundations of the state.[1] Conversely, in Muslim societies, despite the distinctions between the cultic and secular prescriptions of Sharia and Fiqh, Islam is to some extent integrated into various spheres of public life.[2] There is no strict bifurcation of human existence into religious and secular domains. This contrast explains the markedly different approaches to the legal regulation of freedom of expression on religious matters.[3] For instance, in many European countries mockery of religious symbols and open criticism of religious doctrines are not considered offences warranting legal consequences.[4] In contrast, in numerous Muslim countries such actions are deemed serious crimes.[5]

It is noteworthy that several Muslim States have repeatedly raised the issue of formulating an international pact prohibiting insults to religious sanctities and prophets of monotheistic religions at various international forums, including the Inter-Parliamentary Union.[6] However, in the West, such proposals are

1 Cesari, Jocelyne, 'Securitization of Islam in Europe: The Embodiment of Islam as an Exception', in Jocelyne Cesari, ed., *Why the West Fears Islam: An Exploration of Muslims in Liberal Democracies* (New York: Palgrave Macmillan US, 2013), pp. 83–105.

2 See, e.g., Mahmood, Saba, *Religious difference in a secular age: A minority report.* (Princeton University Press, 2015).

3 See, e.g., Himeur, Chihab Mohammed, *Islam et libertés religieuses: le combat des valeurs?* Préface by Bertrand Mathieu. (Brussels: Bruylant, 2022).

4 Dangubić, Marija, Maykel Verkuyten, and Stark, Tobias H., 'Rejecting Muslim or Christian religious practices in five West European countries: a case of discriminatory rejection?' *Ethnic and Racial Studies* 43.16 (2020), pp. 306–326.

5 Ali, Muhammad, Liu Yi Deng Liu, and Khalid, Muhammad Khabeer., 'Legality of Blasphemy in Islam: A Brief Comparison of Legislations around the World', *Islamic Quarterly* 66.1 (2022), pp. 91–130.

6 Marshall, Paul, 'Exporting blasphemy restrictions: The organisation of the Islamic conference and the United Nations', *The Review of Faith & International Affairs* 9.2 (2011), pp. 57–63; Widelitz, Kiley, 'A Global Blasphemy Law: Protecting Believers at the Expense of Free Speech',

perceived as an infringement upon one of the most fundamental rights: freedom of speech and expression.

It can be observed that the relationship between European and Islamic legal cultures is inherently contradictory and frequently assumes the character of acute conflict. The issues discussed in this context are likely to remain pertinent for an extended period. There seems to be no straightforward or unequivocal solution to these problems. Nonetheless, it is possible for the parties involved to mitigate the level of confrontation, avoid direct conflict and pursue avenues for preventing potential exacerbations related to Muslim minorities in the West. It is crucial that these opportunities are effectively utilised.

States Parties to the European Convention address these issues in various ways, which can sometimes result in violations of the fundamental rights of Muslims as guaranteed by the Convention. Accordingly, the European Court of Human Rights acts as the necessary arbiter, tasked with balancing public and private interests.

The European Court of Human Rights has developed criteria for determining violations of religious freedoms in cases involving Muslims, which are crucial for balancing public and private interests within the framework of the European Convention on Human Rights. These criteria are particularly relevant, given the fundamental differences between Islamic and secular legal cultures, and the varied approaches of European States to integrating Muslim practices within their legal systems. The ECtHR's role as an arbiter is pivotal in ensuring that the rights of Muslims are protected while maintaining public order and respecting secular principles.

The following section will provide an overview of ECtHR cases relevant to the topic, focusing on the criteria for determining violations of religious freedoms in cases involving Muslims. Based on existing practice, these can be divided into two categories: Requirements for the Nature of a Religious Community and Its Activities, and Criteria for Determining Religious Affiliation and Its Connection with Violation of Freedom of Conscience.

Pepperdine Policy Review Vol. 6, Article 2 (2013). Сюкияйнен, Леонид. *Ислам и права человека в диалоге культур и религий*. Litres, 2022, p. 181.

1 Requirements for the Nature of a Religious Community and Its Activities

1.1 *Islam-Ittihad Association and Others v. Azerbaijan* (*No. 5548/05*)[7]

1.1.1 Brief Overview of the Facts of the Case

The applicant, the Islam-Ittihad Association, was an Azerbaijani non-governmental organisation operating between 1991 and 2003. It was involved in the restoration of mosques and a number of charitable projects aimed at educating and improving society in the spirit of Islam. In January 1998, at a general meeting of the association's members, it was decided to repair the Juma Mosque in Baku and to develop pilgrimage to this Islamic shrine. The stumbling block was the fact that centring onthe mosque, according to members of the organisation, there was an allegedly illegal monopoly that controlled pilgrimages to Islamic shrines in the country, namely the Department of Caucasian Muslims. The Islam-Ittihad Association launched a media campaign to draw public attention to the problem.

In 2002, the Ministry of Justice issued three warnings to the Association, stating that, in accordance with domestic law, organisations of this type must refrain from engaging in 'religious activities'. Among other things, government agencies had questions about the Association's composition and sources of financing. The organisation did not act as a legal entity and was actually located in the mosque. The Chairman of the Association was also the head of the religious community, and all members of the Association were also members of this community. Government inspectors were unable to determine whether the Association functioned as a non-governmental organisation or as a religious organisation.

In turn, the Association argued that Azerbaijani legislation did not contain any definition of 'religious activity' and that government authorities had not specified which activities fell under the definition of 'religious'. When it continued its activities, the organisation was dissolved in 2003 at the request of the Ministry of Justice. All domestic courts unanimously decided to liquidate it as a non-governmental organisation engaged in religious activities in violation of the law.

Members of the Islam-Ittihad Association lodged a complaint with the ECtHR on the basis of a violation of Articles 10 and 11 of the European Convention on Human and Civil Rights, claiming that the forced dissolution of

7 Islam-Ittihad Association and Others v. Azerbaijan—5548/05—Chamber Judgment [2014] ECHR 1220 (13 November 2014).

the Association violated their rights to freedom of association and freedom of expression.

1.1.2 Position of the Court

The ECtHR found a violation of Article 11 of the Convention. First of all, the Court noted that the right to form an association is an integral part of the right under Article 11 of the Convention. States, according to the Court, although they 'have the right to ensure that the objects and activities of the association are in accordance with the rules established by law, must do so in a manner consistent with their obligations under the Convention' (paragraph 39). The Court further noted the important role of non-political associations for the proper functioning of democracy (paragraph 40).

In its decision on this case, the Court paid great attention to the legislative validity of the actions of the Azerbaijani authorities. Discussing the requirements for legislative technology, the ECtHR noted that the law must be accessible to interested parties and formulated with sufficient precision as to be able—if necessary, with appropriate recommendations—to foresee, to a degree that is reasonable under the circumstances, the consequences that this action may entail (paragraph 43). In the context of the case under consideration, the interference provided for by law was excessive, since at the time of the events Azerbaijani legislation did not contain a definition of religious activity. The national courts, instead of giving their interpretation or drawing the attention of the legislator to the existing lacuna in the law, placed the burden of proof on the Association, ruling that it did not provide any reliable evidence that it was not engaged in such activities (paragraph 22).

Finally, the Court noted that the Ministry and the domestic courts had also failed to indicate what religious activities the Association was allegedly engaged in (paragraph 50). The only evidence relied upon by the national authorities in this regard was the minutes of the general meeting of the Association. It followed that members of the Association discussed, among other things, the organisation of pilgrimages to shrines and the 'monopoly' of the Caucasus Muslims Office in this area. However, the Court indicated that the organisation of pilgrimages to shrines constituted one of the objectives of the Association, as provided for in its Charter, which was registered by the Ministry of Justice (paragraph 8). The Court believed that the fact of this registration and the absence in the case materials of evidence of government requests to amend these provisions of the Charter indicated that representatives of Azerbaijan could not refer to the Association's organisation of pilgrimages as engaging in religious activities. Nor did the Ministry provide any explanation of why it considered the discussion of the above-mentioned matter to be a 'religious activity' (paragraph 50).

Accordingly, the Court considered that the absence of any definition of the term 'religious activity' deprived the applicant of the opportunity to assess what constituted 'religious activity' in order to carry out its activities in accordance with domestic law. Thus, the national authorities were given unlimited discretionary powers in this area (paragraph 51).

1.2 *Kasymakhunov and Saybatalov v. Russia (No. 26261/05 and 26377/06)*[8]

1.2.1 Brief Overview of the Facts of the Case

This is the first ECtHR decision to involve members of Hizb ut-Tahrir in Russia. This case effectively ends any further proceedings in the European Court related to Hizb ut-Tahrir, except for those convicted of acts committed before August 2006, or where there are other issues related to criminal justice in Russia in general.[9]

The applicants were convicted of membership of the radical Islamic organisation Hizb ut-Tahrir al-Islami. Both were serving sentences for committing terrorist crimes. At the time their cases were considered by Russian national courts, as Hizb ut-Tahrir was not officially declared a terrorist organisation. This happened only in 2003, during the Supreme Court's conviction of one of the applicants. The Supreme Court's decision was not published at that time, and the list of banned organisations was officially published only in 2006. The basis of the complaint alleges violations of Articles 9, 10 and 11 of the Convention for having been subjected to criminal penalties for membership of an organisation, spreading its ideology and recruiting new members.

1.2.2 Position of the Court

The Court rejected the applicants' complaints. However, it first referred to the information at its disposal about the nature and activities of Hizb ut-Tahrir (paragraphs 44–47). As a result, the Court found Hizb ut-Tahrir's activities to be contrary to the spirit and values of the European Convention in accordance with its Article 17, and therefore its representatives could not invoke the Con-

---

8 Kasymakhunov and Saybatalov v. Russia—26261/05 26377/06—HEJUD [2013] ECHR 217 (14 March 2013).

9 European Human Rights Advocacy Centre (EHRAC), 'Kasymakhunov and Saybatalov v. Russia,' European Human Rights Advocacy Centre. https://ehrac.org.uk/ru/key-ehrac-cases/kasymakhunov-saybatalov-v-russia/.

vention in a situation in which their criminal prosecution was conditioned by membership of it (paragraph 104).

Article 17 of the European Convention on Human Rights—Prohibition of abuse of rights

Nothing in this Convention may be interpreted as implying for any State, group or person any right to engage in any activity or perform any act aimed at the destruction on any of the rights and freedoms set forth herein or at their limitation to a greater extent than is provided for in the Convention

Importantly, the Court determined the limits to which political organisations can continue to benefit from the protection of the Convention in carrying out their activities. It has been established that a political organisation can contribute to changing the law or the legal and constitutional structure of the State under two conditions: first, the means used for this purpose must be legal and democratic; secondly, the proposed changes must themselves be compatible with fundamental democratic principles (paragraph 105).

In the case of Hizb ut-Tahrir, the organisation's failure to comply with the Court's limits lay in its statements calling for violence against Jews and its readiness to use this violence (paragraph 107). In addition, the Court pointed to the desire of the terrorist association's leadership to gain political power in order to overthrow non-Muslim governments and impose Islamic rule throughout the world, rejecting any possibility of participation in the democratic political process (paragraph 108). This programme involves the introduction of a distinction between people in all areas of private and public law, with different rights and freedoms being granted to them depending on their religion (paragraph 110). The most Court's important conclusion in the case under consideration concerned the incompatibility of the ideals of democracy and Sharia (paragraph 111).

The Court stated that the applicants sought to invoke Articles 9, 10 and 11 to provide a basis under the Convention for the right to engage in activities contrary to the Convention's text and spirit. If this right were granted to them, it would contribute to the destruction of the rights and freedoms set out in the Convention and mentioned above. It followed that the applicants' complaints under Articles 9, 10 and 11 were incompatible with the provisions of the Convention within the meaning of Article 35 § 3 (a) and had to be rejected.

of Article 35(3) of the European Convention on Human Rights—Admissibility criteria

3. The Court shall declare inadmissible any individual application submitted under Article 34 if it considers that:
(a) the application is incompatible with the provisions of the Convention or the Protocols thereto, manifestly ill-founded, or an abuse of the right of individual application; or
(b) the applicant has not suffered a significant disadvantage, unless respect for human rights as defined in the Convention and the Protocols thereto requires an examination of the application on the merits.

1.3 *Bektashi Community and Others v. The Former Yugoslav Republic of Macedonia (No. 48044/10, 75722/12 and 25176/13)*[10]

1.3.1 Brief Overview of the Facts of the Case

The Bektashi Community Association, whose representatives belonged to one of the branches of Sufi Islam, had operated in the Yugoslav Republic of Macedonia as an officially recognised religious organisation since 1993. When new Macedonian legislation on the legal status of churches, religious communities and groups came into force in 2007, the association asked the registration court to recognise its legal status. The request was rejected due to the fact that, by virtue of the new law, confirmation of the status of a religious organisation was possible only for organisations registered before 1998. The Bektashi Community Association was included in the national list of religious organisations only in 2000.

For this reason, the association submitted a new application for registration under the new legislation, but in 2010 this request was also rejected, mainly because the courts concluded that its name and doctrinal sources were identical to the names and doctrinal sources of another already registered religious organisation, a fact which might cause confusion among believers. This 'identical' religious organisation was the religious group Ehlibeit Bektashi of Macedonia, registered in 2010 during the period of disputes between the applicants and the government.

Relying in particular on Article 9 (freedom of thought, conscience and religion) and Article 11 (freedom of assembly and association) of the European Convention, the applicants complained about the decisions of the domestic

10 Bektashi Community and Others v. The Former Yugoslav Republic of Macedonia—48044/10 [2018] ECHR 325 (12 April 2018).

courts refusing to recognise the association as a religious organisation or to re-register it.

1.3.2 Position of the Court

The Court found a violation of Article 11 in the light of Article 9 of the Convention in respect of the applicant association (paragraph 46). The Court noted that the main complaint was the inability of a religious organisation to maintain its status and act collectively in the religious sphere (paragraph 54).

Since, according to the Court, the basis for refusing to re-register the applicant association was purely formal—specifically that it had not been registered by the Commission as a religious organisation until 1998 and was included in the list only in 2000—and since the government, as the respondent, had failed to provide any legal grounds for the refusal, the interference with the applicant association's rights to freedom of association and religion could not be deemed 'necessary in a democratic society'. There has thus been a violation of Article 11 of the Convention, read in the light of Article 9, on account of the domestic authorities' refusal to recognise the applicant association's continuing status as a religious organisation (paragraphs 65–66).

In the context of the religious identity of the applicants and the religious organisation registered in 2010, the Court refrained from any comparison between their religious doctrines. In the Court's view, the domestic courts' assessment and interpretation of the fundamental principles of the applicant association's faith were incompatible with the State's role as a neutral and impartial organiser of the exercise of different religions, creeds and beliefs, 'which excludes, except in very exceptional cases, any discretion of the State in assessing the legality of religious beliefs or ways of expressing those beliefs' (paragraph 72). Also, the European Court was not convinced by the respondent State's argument about the need to prevent religious conflicts (paragraph 73).

1.3.3 Intermediate Conclusions

The Convention bodies lack authority to define religion, yet it should be interpreted liberally.[11] Religious beliefs extend beyond mainstream faiths, requiring identifiability, though the applicant's self-identification is valued when facing government intrusion. Case law on major religions was scant due to established doctrines and state relations. However, the treatment is more sensitive

11 Clause 11 of the Overview of the ECHR's Case-Law on Freedom of Religion, 2013. *Kronadaran*. https://kronadaran.am/wp-content/uploads/2015/02/Overview-of-the-ECtHR-Case-Law-on-Freedom-of-Religion.pdf.

for minority and new religious groups, often labelled 'sects'. Present Court jurisprudence ensures equal protection for all religious groups and adherents under the Convention, promoting tolerance and non-discrimination.

Analysing the above cases, we can highlight the following principles of the ECtHR, which it applies in resolving disputes involving religious associations. Key requirements include the presence of clear legislative formulations or judicial definitions of religion, the prohibition of extremism and terrorism in religious organisations, and the preservation of social harmony and democracy through non-interference by the State in religious matters.

One fundamental requirement established by the ECtHR is the necessity for clear legislative formulations or judicial definitions regarding religion and religious activity. The case of *Islam-Ittihad Association and others v. Azerbaijan* emphasises the importance of legal clarity in defining religious organisations and their activities. Clear definitions provide guidance for both religious communities and State authorities, preventing ambiguity and ensuring that religious freedoms are respected within a coherent legal framework.

Another crucial requirement emphasised by the ECtHR is the inadmissibility of extremism and terrorism in the activities of religious organisations. In cases such as *Kasymakhunov and Saybatalov v. Russia*, the ECtHR reaffirmed its stance against extremism, stating that religious freedoms had to be exercised within the bounds of law, public order and national security. The ECtHR prohibits terrorist organisations from invoking the European Convention to justify their activities, emphasising its commitment to protecting individual rights while upholding broader societal interests.

Additionally, the ECtHR emphasises the preservation of social harmony and democracy by refraining from interfering in religious matters and banning recognised religious organisations. In *Bektashi Community and Others v. The former Yugoslav Republic of Macedonia*, the ECtHR reiterated the principle that the State should not assess the content of a particular religion. Instead, the State should promote tolerance, pluralism and respect for religious diversity, allowing individuals and communities to practise their faith freely.

2 Criteria for Determining Religious Affiliation and iTs Connection with Violation of Freedom of Conscience

2.1 *Sinan Işık v. Turkey* (No. 21924/05)

2.1.1 Brief Overview of the Facts of the Case

The applicant belonged to the Alevi religious community. In 2004, he applied to the domestic courts to have his religious affiliation indicated on his identity card as 'Alevi' rather than 'Muslim', but this was rejected. In 2006, a law was passed that made it possible to leave the 'religion' column on an identity card blank or remove it altogether. However, the applicant considered this to be insufficient. In his opinion, if identity cards provided for an indication of religion, the very fact of leaving the corresponding column blank inevitably acquired a hidden meaning. On this basis the applicant complained that Turkish law forced him to disclose his religious beliefs.

The applicant therefore considered that there had been a violation of Article 9 of the Convention on account of the State authorities' refusal to indicate the applicant's (Alevi) religion on his identity document and the very fact that his identity document contained an indication of religion, regardless of whether it was mandatory or optional.

2.1.2 Position of the Court

The Court found a violation of Article 9 of the European Convention. In justifying its position, the Court noted that while religious freedom is primarily a matter of individual conscience, it also implies the freedom to manifest one's religion alone, privately or in community with others, publicly and among those whose faith one shares. Moreover, the Court further stated that Article 9 enshrines negative rights, such as the freedom not to hold religious beliefs or to profess a religion (paragraph 38).

In this regard, the Court, relying on its jurisprudence in a similar case *Sofianopoulos and Others v. Greece* (No. 1977/02, 1988/02 and 1997/02, ECtHR 2002-X) came to the conclusion that the right to manifest one's religion or belief also had a negative aspect, namely the right of a person not to be obliged to disclose his or her religion or beliefs and not to be obliged to act in a way that would lead to an inference that he or she held—or did not hold—such beliefs. Therefore, public authorities did not have the right to interfere with a person's freedom of conscience and to attempt to disclose his or her religious beliefs or to compel him or her to disclose such beliefs (paragraph 41).

The Court also found a violation of the applicant's rights by the fact that his religious affiliation was assessed by the national authorities on the basis of an opinion issued by the body responsible for Islamic religious affairs (paragraph 46). This, in the Court's opinion, violated the State's duty to maintain neutrality and impartiality.

Based on these findings, it was concluded that the legislative changes introduced in 2006 could not possibly change the situation, since ID cards still contained a field for religion—regardless of whether it was left blank or not. Additionally, the Court found that anyone wishing to change the information about their religion indicated on their identity card had to submit a written application. This fact (the obligation to submit an application to exclude a religion from civil registries), together with the need frequently to present a document containing information about the holder's religion, indirectly forces the applicant to disclose information about his attitude to religion (paragraphs 50 and 51).

However, the Court noted that the violation in question arose not from the failure to indicate the applicant's (Alevi) religion on his identity card, but from the problem of indicating—mandatorily or optionally—his religion on the identity card (paragraph 52). There had thus been a violation of Article 9 of the Convention.

Although the majority of judges voted to uphold the appeal, Judge Cabral Baretto issued a dissenting opinion in which he criticised the Court's position.

First of all, Judge Baretto noted that the applicant's complaint suggested three possible options for resolving this problem:

- the applicant's request to replace the word 'Islam' with 'Alevi' to indicate his religion;
- or, alternatively, a request to remove the indication of religion, in this case 'Islam', from his identity document;
- removal of the 'religion' column from the identity card.

Following the passage of the law allowing the exclusion of religious affiliation, complaints relating to the first two points were eliminated domestically and, therefore, this part of the application should have been excluded from the list (paragraph 2 of the Dissenting Opinion). However, the applicant himself did not raise with the domestic authorities the issue of removing the 'religion' column from the identity card. According to Judge Baretto, this took some of the responsibility from the Turkish government.

The dissenting opinion further noted that requests to remove religious identification from identification documents were not subject to any restrictions but required only a written application (paragraph 3.2 of the Dissenting Opinion). Since a person, when submitting such an application, was not required to disclose his religion or provide any information about his beliefs, there iwasno violation of his right to non-disclosure of his religious affiliation. The reverse interpretation, shared by the majority of the judges, according to Judge Baretto 'goes beyond our case-law and represents an excessive approach, hardly consistent with the margin of appreciation that should be given to states in this area' (paragraph 3.2 of the Dissenting Opinion).

2.2 *Ibragim Ibragimov and Others v. Russia* (*No. 413/08, 28621/11*)[12]

2.2.1 Brief Overview of the Facts of the Case

The applicants were engaged in the publication of books written by the famous Turkish theologian, Said Nursi, and devoted to the interpretation of the Qur'an. Despite the testimony of many Muslim theologians that Said Nursi's books belong to the moderate mainstream of Islam, the Russian authorities recognised these texts as extremist literature, which entailed a ban on their publication and distribution, as well as the subsequent seizure of undistributed copies. The applicants unsuccessfully appealed this decision and appealed to the ECtHR on the grounds of a violation of Articles 9 and 10 of the European Convention.

2.2.2 Position of the Court

The Court found a violation of Article 10 of the Convention. First, it noted that the complaints submitted were subject to consideration only in accordance with Article 10 of the Convention. At the same time, the Court made a reservation that the issues of freedom of expression and freedom of religion were closely related in the present case. This followed from the fact that the books in question contained commentaries on the Qur'an and the applicants intended to use them for religious purposes, including religious education. The case was therefore examined in the light of the Court's case law, including that on issues of freedom of religion (paragraph 78).

The Court also stated that the applicants' complaints were subject to consideration from the point of view alone of the proportionality of the authorities' intervention within the framework of national anti-extremist legislation. The Court therefore left open the question whether the interference with the applicants' right to freedom of expression could be considered 'prescribed by law' within the meaning of Article 10(2) of the Convention (paragraph 86).

Discussing the merits of the case, the Court concluded that there was no extremist content in Said Nursi's books and that the respondent government had no margin of appreciation in this case (paragraphs 101–103).

The Court noted that the domestic courts had made no attempt to conduct their own legal analysis of the texts in question. In particular, in the Court's view, they failed adequately to specify which passages from the book they considered problematic and how they incited religious strife or proclaimed the superiority or inferiority of people on the basis of their relationship to reli-

---

12 Ibragim Ibragimov and Others v. Russia—1413/08 (Judgment: Remainder inadmissible: Third Section), [2018] ECHR 684 (28 August 2018).

gion (paragraphs 107 and 114). The presence in the documents relating to the case of expert conclusions about 'humiliating images, unfavourable and negative assessments of people based on their attitude to religion', from the point of view of the Court, could not in itself mean the extremist orientation of the texts. Nor did the domestic courts discuss the context in which the books were published, their nature and wording, or their potential to cause harmful consequences (paragraph 99).

The Court noted that the fact that portions of text might be perceived as offensive or insulting by individuals or groups did not mean that it constituted 'hate speech' (paragraph 115). The key issue in the present case, therefore, was whether the statements in question, when read as a whole and in their context, could be regarded as advocating violence, hatred or intolerance.

Based on the above reasoning, the Court came to the conclusion that in the framework of the first complaint (No. 1413/08) there was an absolute ban on the publication and distribution of books, since the courts of the Russian Federation did not even indicate which fragments of the text of the books they considered 'extremist'. For this reason, the applicants were not able to re-publish the books after correcting the problematic texts. In the second complaint (No. 28261/11), the Court indicated that Russian courts banned books only because of individual statements, without taking into account the content of the books as a whole.

Moreover, in the Court's opinion, neither the courts nor the authorities of the Russian Federation had referred to any facts that would indicate that the circumstances surrounding the case (its general context) at the material time, such as the presence of interracial tensions or an atmosphere of hostility or hatred between religious communities of the Russian Federation, in which there was a risk that the statements in question could cause an outbreak of violence, serious inter-religious clashes or other similarly serious consequences. From all this it followed that the applicants' rights had been violated.

2.3 *Föderation der Aleviten Gemeinden in Österreich v. Austria (No. 64220/19)*[13]

2.3.1 Brief Review of Actual Circumstances of the Case

This case is somewhat similar to *Bektashi Community and Others v The former Yugoslav Republic of Macedonia*, reviewed above. The applicant was an Alevi religious association in Austria. Its application for recognition as a religious

13 Föderation der Aleviten Gemeinden in Österreich v. Austria—64220/19 [2024] ECHR 195 (5 March 2024).

community was rejected due to the similarity of its statutes with those of another similar religious association. Thus, the Austrian authorities refused to register the religious association on the grounds that it professed the same faith as the members of the already registered one. The amendments to the articles of association also did not facilitate the applicant's registration (paragraph 22).

2.3.2 Position of the Court

The Court found a violation of Article 9 of the Convention. Initially, it recalled the right of a religious community to autonomous existence (paragraph 49). It further stated that the provisions of the Vienna City Law requiring that the statutes of a religious community should include the presentation of a religious doctrine different from that of any registered religious communities were consistent with the Convention and foreseeable (paragraph 54).

However, the Court further considered unacceptable the refusal to register a religious association after it had made changes to its charter and the assessment of these changes by national courts as an abuse of law (paragraphs 56–59).

On the basis of the above arguments, the Court considered that the risk of confusion relied on by the respondent Government could not be a ground for refusing the applicant's registration (paragraphs 62 and 63). Accordingly, there has been a violation of Article 9 of the Convention.

One of the judges did not agree with the majority's conclusion. In his dissenting opinion, Judge Vehabović noted that Article 9 of the Convention does not grant any right to religious organisations to a specific legal status. It simply requires that religious groups be able to acquire legal personality under civil law.

Based on this, Judge Vehabowicz concluded that since Austria already had a registered Alevi religious community, the registration of a new religious community, almost identical to the other in wording and in terms of religious doctrine, did not add any additional value to the right to freedom of religion under Article 9 of the Convention.

2.3.3 Intermediate Conclusions

The European Court of Human Rights employs specific criteria to determine religious affiliation and its nexus to violations of freedom of conscience in cases involving Muslims. Central to these considerations is the recognition of an individual's right to privacy regarding their religious beliefs, as emphasised in *Sinan Işık v. Turkey*. Here, the Court stresses the importance of respecting an individual's choice not to disclose their religious convictions as they see fit, thereby safeguarding their autonomy and privacy rights.

Furthermore, the ECtHR acknowledged the right of individuals to assert the superiority of their religion over that of others, provided that such expression did not incite violence or discrimination against those of differing beliefs. This principle was exemplified in *Ibragim Ibragimov and Others v. Russia*, where the Court emphasised that while individuals might advocate for the pre-eminence of their religious faith, it was impermissible to espouse or promote violence against individuals professing alternative beliefs. This stressed the delicate balance between freedom of expression and the prevention of hate speech or incitement to violence in religious discourse.

In accordance with the ECtHR's stance, national courts are required to conduct comprehensive examinations of sacred texts to assess the potential for incitement to aggression or violence. This necessitates a nuanced understanding of the context in which individual statements are made, taking into account factors such as historical context, rhetorical devices and intended audience. This approach was elucidated in various cases where the Court emphasised the importance of contextual analysis in adjudicating on cases involving religious expression, ensuring a balanced approach that upheld both freedom of religion and the prevention of harm or discrimination.

Additionally, the ECtHR recognised the right of religious groups to maintain autonomy and self-identity, even if they shared similar beliefs and practices with other groups. This principle was affirmed in *Federation der Aleviten Gemeinden in Österreich v. Austria*, where the Court upheld the right of Alevi communities to distinguish themselves from other Muslim denominations, affirming their unique religious identity and autonomy. This shows the importance of respecting diversity within religious communities and upholding their right to self-determination.

CHAPTER 3

Relations between the State and Islam

The relationship between the State and Islam in the practice of the European Court of Human Rights is complex, multifaceted and reflective of the broader challenges faced by European countries in the integration of diverse Muslim populations. The absence of a single hierarchically and territorially organised Islamic body, akin to the Christian Church, combined with the diverse origins of Muslims, presents unique legal and administrative challenges.[1] European states are thus compelled to recognise and regulate a plethora of religious actors who have often had little prior interaction with state authorities.

European countries encounter requests to legalise numerous Islamic religious actors, who can be broadly categorised into three groups:

1. Local, regional and national unions and associations. These entities typically include the terms 'Islamic' or 'Muslim' in their names. They can be the founders of mosques or religious schools and may unite mosques and schools that share an ethnic profile or theological persuasion. *Refah Partisi (The Welfare Party) and Others v. Turkey* (which will be considered by us in the second part of this chapter) illustrates the complexity involved. The ECtHR upheld Turkey's ban on the Welfare Party, which advocated for a legal system based on Sharia law, deeming it incompatible with the principles of democracy.

2. Educational and cultural centres. Often based on ethnic lines, such as Turkish, Arab or Pakistani, these entities engage in educational, missionary and publishing activities. They play a crucial role in maintaining cultural and religious continuity among Muslim communities. However, their activities are closely monitored to ensure compliance with national laws. For instance, the ECtHR has addressed the conflict between individual religious expression and the State's interest in maintaining secularism in educational institutions.

3. Religious and political organisations. These may not always have 'Islamic' in their names but can have significant religious and political characteristics. Some of them may be hostile to democratic constitutional principles. The ECtHR case, *Hizb ut-Tahrir and Others v. Germany*, dealt with an organisation that advocated for the establishment of an Islamic Caliphate, which led to its prohibition by reason of its anti-democratic stance.[2]

---

1 Kuran, Timur, 'The Absence of the Corporation in Islamic Law: Origins and Persistence', *The American Journal of Comparative Law* 53.4 (2005), pp. 785–834.

2 Hizb ut-Tahrir and Others v. Germany—27306/07 [2012] ECHR 1045 (12 June 2012).

The legal framework of European countries generally upholds freedom of opinion, including religious beliefs, as long as it does not incite violence. This principle was evident in the *Gündüz v. Turkey* case (which will be discussed in the second part of Chapter Three), where the ECtHR ruled that statements advocating for Sharia law were protected under the freedom of expression as long as they did not incite violence. However, the Court also maintains a fine balance, emphasising that freedom of expression does not protect hate speech or calls to violence.

The integration of Islamic actors into European legal and social frameworks is a nuanced process. European States must balance the protection of religious freedoms with the need to maintain public order and to uphold democratic values. This is particularly challenging when dealing with organisations or individuals who may have controversial reputations or who advocate for ideologies that conflict with democratic principles.[3]

Turkey's path towards democratisation and integration into the European Union (EU) exemplifies the complexities involved in managing the relationship between the State and Islam. As Turkey navigates this path, it must accommodate moderate Islamic currents while maintaining strict control over radical movements. The pressure exerted by the West, particularly through the EU accession process, has played a crucial role in shaping Turkey's approach to Islam.[4]

The relationship between the State and Islam in the practice of the ECtHR reflects broader societal and legal challenges. European States, bound by the principles of the European Convention on Human Rights, must navigate the complex terrain of religious freedom, public order and democratic values. The ECtHR plays a pivotal role in adjudicating on these issues, ensuring that States strike a balance between respecting religious freedoms and maintaining public order and democratic principles.

In addressing the diversity of Islamic actors and the legal challenges they present, the ECtHR's jurisprudence underscores the importance of context, proportionality and the protection of fundamental rights. This delicate balance is essential for fostering social cohesion and ensuring that the rights of Muslim communities are protected within the broader framework of European legal and social norms. For comparison purposes, we have divided this discussion into two sections based on the religious affiliation of the majority of the coun-

---

3 Tavkhelidze, Tatia, 'Islam and Secularism within the Legal Framework of the European Union', *Journal of the Contemporary Study of Islam* 4.1 (2024), pp. 5–16.

4 For example see Aydın-Düzgit, Senem, and Tocci, Nathalie, *Turkey and the European Union*. London and New York: Palgrave Macmillan, 2015.

tries' populations: the status of Islam, parties and other public and political Islamic organisations in jurisdictions with an Islamic minority and their status in jurisdictions without such an Islamic majority.

1 Status of Islam. Parties and Other Public and Political Islamic Organisations in Jurisdictions with an Islamic Minority

1.1 *Serif v. Greece (No. 38178/97)*[5]

1.1.1 Brief Overview of the Facts of the Case

In 1985, one of the two Muslim religious leaders (muftis) in the Greek region of Thrace died. The State appointed an interim mufti. When he resigned, a second interim mufti was appointed. Throughout this time, elections for a new mufti were not held. In 1990, the President of the Republic finally approved his candidate for the vacant post.

However, two independent Muslim members of parliament then asked the government to organise elections for the post of mufti, as provided for by the law in force at that time. They also demanded that the state organise elections for the post of the second Muslim religious leader of Thrace. Having received no response, independent deputies decided themselves to organise elections in mosques. The applicant in the present case was elected mufti and immediately began to fulfill his duties, which included, among other things, legally significant actions such as registering the marriages of and managing the inheritance affairs of Muslims. A lawsuit was also launched to challenge the legality of the President's appointment of the mufti, bypassing the existing law.

However, shortly before these elections, the government changed the procedure for electing muftis; now the candidacy of a mufti had to be approved by the President. At the beginning of 1991, this law was given retroactive force by the Greek Parliament.

At the end of 1991, criminal proceedings were brought against the applicant for usurping the functions of a minister of a 'known religion' and for publicly wearing the garb of such a minister without having the right to do so.

The applicant, believing that his conviction was not necessary in a democratic society and that the government had discriminated against Muslims compared to members of other religions who had the right to elect their religious leaders, complained to the ECtHR about a violation of Articles 9 and 10 of the Convention.

---

5 Serif v. Greece—38178/97 [1999] ECHR 169 (14 December 1999).

1.1.2 Position of the Court

The Court found a violation of Article 9 of the Convention. First, the court noted that the domestic courts which sentenced the applicant did not mention in their decisions any specific actions of the applicant. The domestic courts found the applicant guilty of the following established charges: distributing a message about the religious significance of a holiday, delivering a speech at a religious meeting, issuing another message on the occasion of a religious holiday and appearing in public dressed as a religious leader (paragraph 51).

Moreover, the Court pointed to the fact that the applicant enjoyed the support of the Muslim community in his region. In the Court's opinion, punishing a person for simply acting as the religious leader of a group that voluntarily followed him could hardly be considered compatible with the requirements of religious pluralism in a democratic society.

The Court rejected the defendant government's argument that, in the particular circumstances of the case, the authorities had to intervene to avoid creating tension among Muslims and between Muslims and Christians in Greek Thrace. The Court stated that the role of the authorities in such circumstances is not to eliminate the cause of tension by eliminating pluralism, but to ensure that competing groups tolerate each other (paragraph 53). The Court continued by pointing out that the government did not provide any evidence of unrest among Muslims, or among Muslims and Christians in the region.

Due to the lack of 'pressing social need', the government's actions were not necessary in a democratic society and violated Article 9 of the Convention.

1.2 *Supreme Holy Council of the Muslim Community v. Bulgaria (No. 39023/97)*[6]

1.2.1 Brief Overview of the Facts of the Case

In Bulgaria after the establishment of a democratic regime there were two separate competing Muslim communities, each with its own leader. However, according to the law, it was possible to register only one nationwide Muslim community. Until 1997, the applicant, the Supreme Sacred Council of the Muslim Community of Bulgaria, was responsible for the administration of the Muslim community in Bulgaria, facing opposition from another competing organisation.

As long as the country was led by the Bulgarian Socialist Party, which supported the applicant, his position remained unshakable. However, the new demo-

6 Supreme Holy Council of the Muslim Community v. Bulgaria—39023/97 [2004] ECHR 690 (16 December 2004).

cratic government that came after the elections, among which were opponents of the applicant, decided to organise a national conference to elect a single leader of the Muslims of Bulgaria. Despite the protests of the Supreme Holy Council of the Muslim Community of Bulgaria, the conference took place and its opponents, supported by the new government, won.

On this basis, the applicant alleged that he was the victim of arbitrary and discriminatory State interference in the organisation of the official Muslim community in Bulgaria. He also argued that the requirements of impartiality and fairness had been violated during the subsequent proceedings. Violations of Articles 6, 9, 13 and 14 of the Convention were alleged.

Article 6 of the European Convention on Human Rights—Right to a fair trial

1. In the determination of his civil rights and obligations or of any criminal charge against him, everyone is entitled to a fair and public hearing within a reasonable time by an independent and impartial tribunal established by law. Judgment shall be pronounced publicly but the press and public may be excluded from all or part of the trial in the interests of morals, public order or national security in a democratic society, where the interests of juveniles or the protection of the private life of the parties so require, or to the extent strictly necessary in the opinion of the court in special circumstances where publicity would prejudice the interests of justice.
2. Everyone charged with a criminal offence shall be presumed innocent until proved guilty according to law.
3. Everyone charged with a criminal offence has the following minimum rights:
(a) to be informed promptly, in a language which he understands and in detail, of the nature and cause of the accusation against him;
(b) to have adequate time and facilities for the preparation of his defence;
(c) to defend himself in person or through legal assistance of his own choosing or, if he has not sufficient means to pay for legal assistance, to be given it free when the interests of justice so require;
(d) to examine or have examined witnesses against him and to obtain the attendance and examination of witnesses on his behalf under the same conditions as witnesses against him;
(e) to have the free assistance of an interpreter if he cannot understand or speak the language used in court.

Article 13 of the European Convention on Human Rights—Right to an effective remedy

Everyone whose rights and freedoms as set forth in this Convention are violated shall have an effective remedy before a national authority notwithstanding that the violation has been committed by persons acting in an official capacity.

1.2.2 Position of the Court

The Court found a violation of Article 9 of the Convention. Citing its own jurisprudence, it held that State measures that favour a particular leader or group in a divided religious community, or that seek to force the community or part of it to submit to a single leadership against its will, constitute a violation of the freedom of religion (for example, as in *Serif v. Greece*) (paragraph 75). In the Court's opinion, the present case concerned the change of leadership of the Bulgarian Muslim community in October 1997 and the subsequent proceedings. It followed that the central point of contention was whether these events were the result of unjustified pressure from the State or nothing more than a change in leadership voluntarily brought about by the community.

According to the Government, the Directorate of Religious Affairs and local authorities participated in the process by encouraging the two groups to unite, mediating between the opposing groups and facilitating the unification process because they had a constitutional duty to ensure religious tolerance and peaceful relations between groups of believers (paragraphs 78 and 79).

However, the Court noted that the process of unification of the Muslim communities in 1997 took place against the backdrop of events in previous years, when a change of government was quickly followed by state action to replace religious leaders and grant legal recognition to one of two competing religious leaders. With a law requiring unified religious leadership, the legal regulation left religious leaders with no choice but to compete for recognition by the current government, with each leader offering to 'unite' the faithful under their leadership (paragraph 81).

Since the Government did not explain why, in this case, its goal of restoring the rule of law and redressing injustice could not be achieved by other means, that is, without forcing a divided community to be under a single leadership, the Court concluded that the Bulgarian authorities had exceeded their margin of appreciation, provided for in Article 9(2) of the Convention (paragraphs 97–98).

1.3 *Georgian Muslim Relations and Others v. Georgia (No. 24225/19)*[7]

1.3.1 Brief Overview of the Facts of the Case

In 2014, the non-profit organisation, Georgian Muslim Relations (GMR), acquired the rights to a building and land in the Georgian city of Kobuleti, intending to open a Muslim boarding school. However, the organisation faced resistance from the local Orthodox community. Its representatives shouted Islamophobic insults near the school's construction site and threatened representatives of the Muslim organisation. The construction and opening of the school were also obstructed. Although members of the Muslim community called the police, upon arrival they simply remained in their cars or stated that they would not intervene unless there was a physical confrontation.

However, by September 2015 the school was ready to open. Then the protesters began more actively to shout insults at school staff, parents and students and began to threaten them with physical harm. One day, after the police had advised Muslims present to leave the school grounds, members of the Orthodox Christian community nailed a bloody pig's head to the school door and threatened to fill the area with pigs. Protesters erected a wooden and tyre barricade and a large white cross at the entrance to the school and held ongoing protests outside, including holding congregational Christian prayers. Over the next two months, protesters controlled who could enter and remain in the school by intimidating or threatening those associated with it. Although the police were also almost constantly present in the area around the school, they did not intervene at any stage. In the end, the opening of the school was disrupted.

The organisation appealed to the ECtHR on the basis of a violation of Articles 3, 8, 9 and 14 of the Convention.

Article 3 of the European Convention on Human Rights—Prohibition of torture

No one shall be subjected to torture or to inhuman or degrading treatment or punishment.

1.3.2 Position of the Court

The Court found that Articles 8 and 9 of the Convention had been violated. Since the acts complained of were committed by private individuals and there-

7 Georgian Muslim Relations and Others v. Georgia—24225/19 [2023] ECHR 949 (30 November 2023).

fore could not be directly attributed to the respondent State, the Court set out to examine the issues from the point of view of the positive obligation of public authorities to ensure that persons within their jurisdiction enjoyed the rights under Article 9 (paragraph 82). In the Court's view, there was a conflict between two sets of competing fundamental rights: the right of the demonstrators to freedom of expression and peaceful assembly, and the right of believers to practise their faith. To determine the balance between these fundamental rights, the Court set out three principles on which States had to rely when resolving such complex issues (paragraph 83).

First, the Court stated that the State has an obligation to ensure, as far as is reasonably possible, the protection of both sets of rights. Secondly, it is necessary to create an effective legal framework. And third, when assessing police responses to contested events, the police's positive obligation to guarantee the rights of both demonstrators and believers must be interpreted in a way that does not impose an impossible or disproportionate burden on them (believers and protesters).

During the proceedings, the Court was of the view that the respondent State had not given due consideration to how to strike an appropriate balance in ensuring respect for the effective exercise of the rights of individual applicants and protesters. Thus, the government had essentially failed to prove how the State protected the applicants' rights (paragraph 86). As regards the role of the police in the events that unfolded, the Court noted that they, having been informed of the ongoing protests, made no effort to identify and punish the leaders of the bullying tactics, ignoring the danger posed by the mob's violent attacks on individuals (paragraphs 90 and 92).

The Court also held that, having regard to the circumstances of the present case, the domestic authorities were faced with *prima facie* signs of incitement to hatred, threats and degrading treatment motivated by the religious beliefs of individual applicants and, according to the Court's case law, this required the effective application of domestic criminal law mechanisms capable of clarifying a possible hate motive behind violent incidents and to identify and, if necessary, adequately punish those responsible (paragraph 93).

As a result, the lack of police intervention resulted in religiously motivated violent acts taking place without any legal consequences, and the applicants were not provided with the necessary protection against interference with their privacy, dignity and religious beliefs. In the light of these findings, the Court concluded that there had been a violation of the positive obligations of the respondent State under Articles 8 and 9 of the Convention taken in conjunction with Article 14.

1.3.3 Intermediate Conclusions

The European Court of Human Rights has developed a robust jurisprudence concerning the rights of parties and other public and political Islamic organisations in jurisdictions with Islamic minorities. Central to this jurisprudence is the protection of religious freedom and the prevention of discrimination based on religious affiliation. The ECtHR's rulings emphasise the fundamental principles of freedom of association, non-discrimination and autonomy within religious communities.

One key aspect of the ECtHR's practice is the principle that individuals cannot be punished solely for engaging in religious activities, even if they do not hold formal leadership positions within a religious group. This principle was reaffirmed in *Serif v. Greece*, where the Court held that individuals have the right freely to practise their religion without fear of reprisal or persecution, regardless of their specific role within a religious organisation.

Furthermore, the ECtHR has consistently held that states cannot impose uniform governance structures on religious groups, even if they share similarities in belief or practice. In *Supreme Holy Council of the Muslim Community v. Bulgaria*, the Court ruled that the State's interference with the organisational processes of a religious group violated the principle of religious autonomy guaranteed under the European Convention on Human Rights. This decision stresses the importance of respecting the internal governance and decision-making processes of religious communities, without undue interference from the State.

In conclusion, States Parties to the Convention have a duty to uphold the rights of individuals and religious groups to the freedoms of association, non-discrimination and autonomy in accordance with the principles established by the ECtHR. These include refraining from punishing individuals for engaging in religious activities, respecting the organisational autonomy of religious groups, and refraining from condoning ongoing oppression or discrimination against representatives of religious communities. By adhering to these principles, States can ensure the protection of religious freedom and promote social harmony and cohesion in multicultural societies.

2 Status of Islamic Minorities, Parties and Other Public and Political Organisations in Jurisdictions with an Islamic Majority

2.1 *Refah Partisi (The Welfare Party) and Others v. Turkey (No. 41340/98, 41342/98, 41343/98 and 41344/98)*[8]

2.1.1 Brief Overview of the Facts of the Case

The Refah Party was a political party in Turkey whose ideology could be described as Islamic conservatism. The 1995 general elections made Refah the largest political party in Turkey, and in 1996 it came to power, forming a coalition government.

The coalition government, led by party leader Refah Necmettin Erbakan, was removed from power by the Turkish military in 1997 due to suspicions that the party was pursuing a political programme to Islamise Turkish society. In 1998, the Turkish Constitutional Court dissolved the Refah Party as 'a center of activities contrary to the principle of secularism' and banned six of its leaders from political party activities for five years.

Representatives of the dissolved party argued that the dissolution of Refah by the Constitutional Court and the suspension of certain political rights of the applicants, who were leaders of Refah, violated Articles 9, 10, 11, 14, 17 and 18 of the European Convention.

Article 18 of the European Convention on Human Rights—Limitation on use of restrictions on rights

The restrictions permitted under this Convention to the said rights and freedoms shall not be applied for any purpose other than those for which they have been prescribed.

2.1.2 Position of the Court

The Court found no violations of the Convention in this case. It noted that the applicants had not provided sufficient evidence to establish that the Refah Party had been dissolved for reasons other than those stated by the Turkish Constitutional Court. Having regard to the importance of the principle of secularism for the democratic system in Turkey, the Court considered that the dissolution of Refah pursued several legitimate aims, namely the protection of national and public security, the prevention of disorder or crime and the protection of the rights and freedoms of citizens (paragraph 67).

8 Refah Partisi (The Welfare Party) and Others v. Turkey—41340/98;41342/98;41343/98 [2001] ECHR 495 (31 July 2001).

The Court gave reasons for its position by stating that the freedoms guaranteed by Article 11, as well as Articles 9 and 10 of the Convention, cannot deprive a State in which a political association, through its activities, endangers the institutions of that State, of the very right to defend these institutions (paragraphs 96–99).

In this context, the Court expressed the view that totalitarian movements organised in the form of political parties can end democracy after prospering under a democratic regime. There are examples of this in modern European history. To combat such movements, the State has the right to use emergency measures, without waiting for the party to come to power and destroy the democratic order, even if such goals are not reflected in its policy documents (paragraphs 100–103).

To determine whether a political party is likely to undermine the democratic order of a country, the Court proposed using the following criteria:

> (i) whether there was plausible evidence that the risk to democracy, supposing it had been proved to exist, was sufficiently imminent; (ii) whether the acts and speeches of the leaders and members of the political party concerned were imputable to the party as a whole; and (iii) whether the acts and speeches imputable to the political party formed a whole which gave a clear picture of a model of society conceived and advocated by the party which was incompatible with the concept of a "democratic society".; (paragraph 104).

The Court found that the activities of the Rafah Party fell within these criteria. Thus, based on the statements of party members who were members of parliament, the Court concluded that the party's main intention was the establishment of a political regime based on Sharia (paragraph 120). In the Court's opinion, the remarks and positions of the Refah leaders formed a coherent whole and gave a clear picture of the model of state and society organised by religious rules conceived and proposed by the party (paragraph 122). In this context, the Court made the crucial statement that:

> Sharia is incompatible with the fundamental principles of democracy as set out in the Convention (paragraph 123).

Let us recall that a similar conclusion was made in *Kasymakhunov and Saybatalov v. Russia* (No. 26261/05 and 26377/06).

Thus, the decision to dissolve the party was correct and legal, since it was aimed at protecting democracy from a movement based on religious fundamentalism. The Grand Chamber's decision marks an important departure from ECtHR case law regarding the dissolution of political parties in the Turkish legal order. In previous cases where parties were dissolved primarily on the grounds that provisions of their Constitution or programme, or public statements made on behalf of the party, served to undermine the integrity or unity of the Republic of Turkey, the ECtHR had always found that there was a violation of Article 11 of the Convention.

However, there was not complete unanimity among the judges considering this case. A number of them, although expressing support for the decision, nevertheless considered it necessary to clarify their position. The concurring opinion of Judges Ress and Rozakis noted that in interpreting paragraphs 97 and 98 of the decision, where the Court referred to the limits on which political movements can continue to rely in the protection of the Convention, it should not be understood to mean that the protection of the Convention was limited to situations where a political party operated in full accordance with the law. In other words, a political party that has committed minor violations of the law retained the right to protection under the Convention from sanctions imposed on it, and in particular from dissolution.

In another concurring opinion, Judge Kovler expressed the opinion that the use of political terms such as 'Islamic fundamentalism' (paragraph 94), 'totalitarian movements' (paragraph 99), 'threat to the democratic regime' (paragraph 107) etc. were vague. He also noted that the Court, in the context of discussing Sharia norms, had not fully analysed the concept of pluralism of legal systems (paragraph 119), which 'is associated with the concept of legal pluralism and is generally recognized'.

2.2 *Erbakan v. Turkey (No. 59405/00)*[9]

This case is related to the previous one.

2.2.1 Brief Overview of the Facts of the Case

The applicant, Necmettin Erbakan, was a Turkish politician and, in particular, was Prime Minister of Turkey from June 1996 to June 1997. At the time in question, he was chairman of the Refah Party (The Welfare Party), which was dissolved in 1998 for engaging in activities contrary to the principles of secularism.

On 25 February 1994, during the local election campaigns, the applicant made a public speech. There was no official record of the performance. More

9 Erbakan vs Turkey—59405/00 (6 July 2006).

than four years later, in July 1998, criminal proceedings were brought against him for inciting hatred and enmity through comments made in his 1994 speech about differences between religions, races and regions. For example, he was accused of criticising other parties, in which he called their representatives infidels and opposing the Qur'an and Allah.

The applicant alleged a violation of Article 10 of the Convention for the restriction of his freedom of expression by the national authorities.

2.2.2 Position of the Court

The Court found a violation of Article 10 of the Convention. It said that the applicant's remarks at the 1994 rally—'if indeed they were made'—could be attributed to an attempt to formulate a political line on the basis of religious affiliation (paragraph 62). However, the Court did not find that the speech gave rise to any of the risks or imminent dangers to society alleged by the respondent Government (paragraph 48).

The Court stated that the rather long period of time, namely four years and five months, that had elapsed between the alleged dissemination of the alleged comments and the initiation of criminal proceedings indicated that the charges were politically motivated and that there was no real threat in the applicant's words (paragraph 68). For this reason, there had been a violation of Article 10 of the Convention.

One of the judges disagreed with the majority opinion. In his partially dissenting opinion, Judge Steiner stated that the applicant's controversial speech was delivered during a public meeting in a region whose population had recently been the victim of terrorist attacks carried out by an extremist organisation. According to the case file, the applicant publicly called on all who considered themselves 'believers' to use violence against those who were not. For this reason, his words had to be considered hate speech, an apology for violence or incitement to violence, which was contrary to the spirit of the Convention and could not be considered merely part of a political debate.

Judge Steiner noted that, in general, this position was shared by the majority. Thus, in paragraph 62 of the decision, the Court recognised that the applicant's statements could be considered incitement to hatred. And although the charge was brought against him after a significant period of time, this was no basis for recognising his criminal prosecution as a violation of Article 10 of the Convention, since this characterises the activities of the prosecutor, but not the essence of the statement, which undermines pluralism and democracy.

In Judge Steiner's opinion, the domestic authorities acted within the limits of their discretion and, given that the applicant never served a prison sentence, the sanction imposed in the present case in the form of a fine and a ban on political activity could not be considered disproportionate to the legitimate aim pursued, namely preventing public incitement to hatred.

2.3 *Izzettin Doğan and Others v. Turkey (No. 62649/10)*[10]

2.3.1 Brief Overview of the Facts of the Case

In this case, representatives of the Shi'i minority—Alevi—again turned to the ECtHR to protect their rights. The applicants—Izzettin Doğan and other members of the Alevi community (collectively referred to as Alevi) (plaintiffs)—filed a case against the Turkish authorities in the ECtHR, arguing that the Turkish government has not sufficiently protected the right of the Alevi to practise their faith. Thus, the Alevi were denied being able to call their faith a distinct religion. For this reason, the religious community could not enjoy the rights of a religious organisation: to receive state religious services in the form of Alevi rites, its leaders were not considered by the State as civil servants, Alevi ceremonial sites did not have the status of places of worship, and also they could not receive government subsidies.

The government argued that the Alevi faith was not a religion like Sunni Islam but was a mystical group within the Islamic faith. Alevi claimed that the government favoured the Sunni majority and discriminated against Alevi and other religious minority groups without any reasonable grounds. Thus, the Alevi claimed a violation of Article 9 of the European Convention.

2.3.2 Position of the Court

The Court voted by a majority that there had been a violation of Article 9 of the Convention. It first stated that, in accordance with Article 9 of the Convention, the right to freedom of thought, conscience and religion applied, of course, only to beliefs which achieved a sufficient degree of force, seriousness, consistency and importance (paragraph 68). And since in the present case neither party denied the existence of a large Alevi community in Turkey (paragraph 36), the essence of the dispute boiled down to the admissibility of the Turkish authorities' assessment of the Alevi community as a religious movement within Islam (paragraph 91).

The Court considered that the alleged refusal, which amounted to a denial of the religious character of the Alevi faith, constituted an interference with the applicants' right to freedom of religion guaranteed by Article 9(1) of the Convention (paragraph 95 of the decision). Moreover, the principle of secularism proclaimed by the Turkish constitution, according to the Court, prohibited the

10 Izzettin Doğan and Others v. Turkey—62649/10 [2016] ECHR 387 (26 April 2016).

State from showing preference for a particular religion or belief (paragraph 115). In this regard, the Court recalled that, in accordance with the legal principle of the autonomy of religious communities, only the highest spiritual authorities of a religious community, and neither the State nor even the national courts could determine to what faith a person belonged (paragraph 121). Because of this, the State's attitude towards the Alevi faith infringed the Alevi community's right to autonomous existence, which underlay the guarantees of Article 9 of the Convention.

An important aspect, specifically emphasised by the Court, was that the applicants did not complain about the absence or unclear nature of the procedure by which Alevism could be recognised as a religious group or denomination (paragraphs 115–116), but precisely about the refusal of such recognition, which placed them in an unequal position with representatives of traditional Islam (paragraph 167). This was considered by the Court to be the Turkish government's main violation.

Some judges considered it necessary to express their dissenting opinion in the case. Thus, in their partially dissenting opinion, Judges Villiger, Keller and Kjölbro noted the absence of a violation of Article 9 of the Convention. In their opinion, the Court ignored the essence of the applicants' complaint, which contained specific demands, and not an abstract accusation that the government did not recognise their religion. Thus, the dissenting Judges noted that Article 9 of the Convention cannot be interpreted as imposing a positive obligation on the State to provide religious services to a religious group, to recognise its places of worship, to employ and pay the salaries of the religious leaders of the group and to allocate funds from the general budget for fully or partially funding group activities. Such an interpretation of Article 9 of the Convention would go too far.

Judge Vehabovich also issued a critical dissenting opinion. He, like the other dissenting judges, noted that substantively none of the applicants' claims had any impact on the applicants' freedom to practise Islam in their own way. In addition, he noted that the Turkish authorities' assessment of the religious nature of Alevi practice in Islam does not amount to a denial that Alevi religious practice constitutes a form of religious worship, nor does it amount to denying the Alevi places of religious assembly or their religious leaders legal protection. The question came down only to state support of Alevism.

2.3.3 Intermediate Conclusions

Maintaining the principles of secularism and democracy in societies with an Islamic majority presents a significant challenge due to the intersection of religious beliefs and political governance. In such societies, religion often plays a central role in public life, influencing laws, social norms and cultural practices. Secularism, which advocates for the separation of religion and state, can face resistance in environments where religious authorities exercise significant influence over political decision-making. Furthermore, the concept of democracy may be interpreted differently within Islamic-majority societies, leading to tensions between religious principles and democratic values. While democracy promotes equality, pluralism and individual freedoms, it may clash with traditional Islamic governance structures and interpretations of religious law.

Navigating these complexities requires careful consideration of the rights and freedoms of all individuals, regardless of their religious beliefs. It necessitates fostering dialogue, promoting tolerance, and finding a balance between religious traditions and democratic principles. Despite the challenges, it is essential to make efforts to uphold secularism and democracy in Islamic-majority societies to ensure the protection of fundamental human rights and the advancement of pluralistic societies.

One key aspect of the ECtHR's practice is its approach to banning radical parties in Islamic-majority countries. In *Refah Partisi (The Welfare Party) and Others v. Turkey*, the Court ruled that banning radical parties does not necessarily violate the ECHR. The Court emphasised that democracy is a fundamental value protected by the Convention, and parties that seek to undermine it through the imposition of Sharia law or other radical ideologies may be subject to restrictions. This emphasises the Court's commitment to upholding democratic principles and preventing the erosion of democratic institutions by extremist elements.

Furthermore, the ECtHR has consistently affirmed the principle of secularism and the inadmissibility of Sharia norms in a democratic society. In the *Refah Partisi* case, the Court explicitly stated that Sharia law does not correspond to democracy, indicating that secularism is a core principle of the Convention. This principle serves to protect the rights of individuals to freedom of religion while also safeguarding the secular nature of the State and its institutions. It reflects the Court's stance on the separation of religion and State and its commitment to preserving democratic values in societies with Islamic majorities.

Additionally, the Court has addressed cases involving radical statements made by pro-Islamic politicians and public figures. In *Erbakan v. Turkey*, the Court held that restrictions on freedom of expression are permissible only if such expressions have a negative effect, such as inciting violence or discrimination. This nuanced approach underscores the Court's recognition of the importance of freedom of expression in democratic societies, while also acknowledging the need to balance this freedom with the protection of other rights and values.

In conclusion, the ECtHR has affirmed the autonomy and recognition of religious movements, including Islamic minorities, within the framework of the ECHR. The Court has emphasised the importance of upholding democratic principles, secularism and freedom of expression while addressing complex issues related to religion and politics. By adhering to these principles, the Court seeks to promote tolerance, pluralism and respect for human rights in societies with diverse religious populations. Ultimately, the ECtHR's jurisprudence serves as a guiding framework for ensuring the protection of fundamental rights and freedoms in Islamic-majority jurisdictions.

CHAPTER 4

Anti-terrorism Policy and Islam

Terrorism poses a unique challenge for democratic governments. The temptation to impose draconian measures for the sake of security is ever-present. However, the essence of democracy lies in its commitment to human rights, even when faced with severe threats. Fighting terrorism 'with one hand tied behind your back' becomes a necessary strategy to uphold democratic values.

The criminalisation of radical Islam represents a significant aspect of the jurisprudence of the European Court of Human Rights. This focus encompasses the application of criminal legislation by countries that are party to the European Convention on Human Rights. Radicalism, understood as an extreme, uncompromising commitment to certain ideas, concepts or views aimed at achieving specific social, political or religious goals, is often rooted in aggressive ideologies and calls for decisive action to overhaul existing socio-economic and political systems.[1] Suppressing the activities of individuals who propagate religious extremist ideologies is crucial not only for addressing specific extremist crimes but also for preventing the creation of social environments conducive to the formation and activity of extremist and terrorist groups.

The intricate relationship between anti-terrorism policies and the protection of Muslim rights under the European Court of Human Rights reveals a complex and frequently contentious landscape.[2] Terrorism, in contrast to regular crimes, provokes a heightened response from states, often leading to the declaration of emergencies where national security overrides other rights. This dynamic is particularly apparent when examining human rights infringements linked to anti-terrorism measures compared to standard law enforcement actions.[3]

---

1 Bötticher, Astrid, 'Towards Academic Consensus Definitions of Radicalism and Extremism,' *Perspectives on Terrorism* 11.4 (2017), pp. 73–77.

2 Sikuta, Jan, 'Threats of Terrorism and the European Court of Human Rights,' *European Journal of Migration and Law* 10.1 (2008), pp. 1–10.

3 Müller, Reto, and Greuter, Stéphanie, *Anti-Terrorist Operations and the Right to Life—The European Court of Human Rights Case Law from Gibraltar to Beslan.* (Bern: Editions Weblaw, 2022), p. 4.

In the context of counter-terrorism, governments frequently invoke national security to justify measures that might otherwise be considered excessive or unlawful under normal circumstances. This shift is evident in the application of the derogation clause under the European Convention on Human Rights, allowing states to derogate from certain obligations during emergencies. The interaction between this clause and the relative and absolute rights enshrined in the Convention provides states with additional latitude within their margin of appreciation.

Surveillance and stop-and-search procedures are quintessential anti-terrorism measures. The ECtHR plays a critical role in defining the boundaries of these practices to prevent excessive human rights violations. The necessity for sufficient safeguards in implementing anti-terrorism measures is a recurring theme in the Court's jurisprudence. The ECtHR's decisions emphasise that while states have a duty to protect their citizens from terrorism, this responsibility must be balanced against the protection of individual rights.[4]

The European Court of Human Rights frequently addresses cases involving the promotion of religious extremist ideas, highlighting the challenge of balancing freedom of expression with the need to protect public order and safety. Effectively to counter radicalism and extremism, it is essential to distinguish between speech that promotes extremist ideas and speech that directly or indirectly incites violence or harm. Propaganda, especially in the context of radical ideologies like Islamist extremism, involves the dissemination of ideas that justify violence or radical societal change. However, it is important to note that international law does not permit the criminalisation of all religious expression or extremist ideas but rather focuses on the restriction of speech that incites violence, hatred or discrimination.

The OSCE Office for Democratic Institutions and Human Rights (ODIHR) emphasises that freedom of religion or belief and freedom of expression do not extend to the right to advocate for beliefs that incite violence or hostility. Under international law, particularly the International Covenant on Civil and Political Rights (ICCPR), Article 19 protects the right to freedom of expression but recognises that this right carries with it 'special duties and responsibilities'. Article 20(2) of the ICCPR specifically requires States Parties to prohibit the advocacy of national, racial or religious hatred that constitutes incitement to violence or discrimination. This means that only speech that directly

4 Nussberger, Angelika, 'Terrorizm i prava cheloveka: o pravoprimenitel'noy praktike Evropeyskogo Suda po pravam cheloveka [Terrorism and Human Rights: On the Jurisprudence of the European Court of Human Rights],' *Mezhdunarodnoe pravosudie* 1 (2018), pp. 67–78.

incites violence, hostility or discrimination falls within the scope of restrictions. Advocating for extremist ideas without inciting violence is not a sufficient ground for criminalisation.[5]

In this context, state authorities are urged carefully to assess whether religious or extremist speech is truly inciting violence before resorting to prosecution or other legal restrictions. The ODIHR suggests using the six-part test set out in the Rabat Plan of Action, which helps to determine whether speech crosses the threshold of incitement to hatred or violence. Importantly, the restriction of speech should be narrowly focused on those instances where the speech clearly encourages harmful actions. This approach ensures that only speech that constitutes a direct incitement to violence is subject to legal action, rather than that limiting broader religious or ideological expression that does not pose a clear threat to public order. Thus, international standards require that restrictions on freedom of expression be justified by concrete evidence of harm, with a focus solely on speech that calls for violence or discrimination.

The extent to which anti-terrorism measures can intrude into individuals' privacy is another critical issue. The ECtHR has raised concerns about serious privacy violations, especially as societies increasingly transition to digital life. *Big Brother Watch and Others v. the United Kingdom* illustrates the Court's approach to mass surveillance.[6] The applicants challenged the bulk interception of communications, which the Court found to be lacking in adequate safeguards, thus violating Articles 8 and 10 (freedom of expression) of the ECtHR.

For a better understanding of all the legal problems of the ECtHR's practice in cases of violation of the rights of Muslims in the context of anti-terrorist and anti-extremist activities, we propose to consider the cases in this chapter in two groups. The first is devoted to the general principles of terrorism prevention and their relationship with the basic rights of believers. The second concerns the most specific types of cases related to the conflict between freedom of expression and public safety.

The ECtHR's decisions reflect an ongoing struggle to maintain a balance between national security and the protection of fundamental rights in the digital age. As surveillance technologies become more pervasive, the potential for abuse increases, necessitating robust judicial oversight to protect individual rights.

The ECtHR's jurisprudence reflects this delicate balance. While recognising the imperative of national security, the Court consistently emphasises the

5 *Freedom of Religion or Belief and Security. Policy Guidance.* OSCE/ODIHR, 2019, pp. 37–39.

6 Big Brother Watch and Others v. the United Kingdom—58170/13—Legal Summary [2014] ECHR 178 (7 January 2014).

need to protect fundamental rights. This approach ensures that states do not exploit security concerns to justify unwarranted infringements on individual freedoms. The challenge for the future lies in adapting to new threats and technologies while steadfastly protecting the core principles of human rights.

1 Violation of Muslim Rights in the Context of Terrorism Prevention

1.1 *Ahmet Arslan and Others v. Turkey* (*No. 41135/98*)[7]

1.1.1 Brief Overview of the Facts of the Case

The applicants belonged to a distinct Muslim religious group. In October 1996, they met for a religious ceremony held in a mosque and walked through the streets of the city in the clothing characteristic of their group. They were detained and taken to a police station. Later, criminal proceedings were initiated against them for violating anti-terrorism legislation. The charges were dropped several years later (paragraphs 8–18). At the State Security Court hearing, the court president asked them to remove their turbans in accordance with Turkish judicial custom, which requires men to appear in court with their heads uncovered. They refused to do this, and the State Security Court notified the prosecutor's office about this. The men were charged with violating a law prohibiting the wearing of certain types of religious clothing in public, except for religious ceremonies. They were convicted and were sentenced to pay a fine, and all their subsequent appeals were unsuccessful. Based on this, a group of applicants filed a complaint with the ECtHR regarding a violation of Article 9 of the Convention.

1.1.2 Position of the Court

The Court found a violation of Article 9 of the Convention. It noted that the applicants were ordinary citizens and, as such, could not be subject to any duty of discretion when publicly expressing their religious beliefs (paragraph 48). The Court further concluded that the applicants were punished for the clothing they wore in public places open to everyone, such as public roads or squares. It was therefore not a question of regulating the wearing of religious symbols in public institutions, where respect for neutrality of belief may take precedence over the free exercise of the right to manifest one's religion (paragraph 49). Likewise, the Court saw no evidence in the case file that the applicants posed a

7 Ahmet Arslan and Others v. Turkey—41135/98—Chamber Judgment (French Text) [2010] ECHR 2260.

threat to public order or exerted pressure on others (paragraphs 50–51). Thus, the violation of the applicants' right to freedom of expression was not sufficiently justified under Article 9 of the Convention.

Judge Sayo expressed a concurring opinion. In his view, in the present case the domestic courts had not taken into account the freedom to manifest religion when applying the Criminal Code, and the Government had failed to demonstrate what public order considerations might have given rise to a criminal conviction.

Judge Popovich expressed the opposite opinion. In his view, Article 9 of the Convention did not protect every action motivated or inspired by religion. In this case, the respondent State exercised its margin of appreciation, which was necessary to maintain the regime of constitutional democracy. Judge Popovich noted that the applicants had violated the law on dress code in public places. For this they were sentenced to the minimum possible term, and the authorities immediately replaced it with a small fine.

1.2 *A. and Others v. the United Kingdom (No. 3455/05)*[8]

1.2.1 Brief Overview of the Facts of the Case

The case concerned 11 applicants who were detained by the UK authorities and given high-security detention on suspicion of terrorism under the Anti-terrorism, Crime and Security Act 2001, which was introduced following the terrorist attacks of 11 September 2001. All the applicants were allegedly associated with extremist Islamist terrorist groups, which in turn were affiliated with Al-Qaeda. They were also suspected of financially supporting these terrorist groups through fundraising, fraud or forgery. The applicants' situation was aggravated by the fact that they could not be deported because they faced a risk of ill-treatment in their home country.

For a period of almost two years, each of the applicants was detained as an international terrorist. Two of them were released because they had decided to leave the United Kingdom, three were transferred to a psychiatric hospital and one was released on conditions amounting to house arrest. The remaining eight applicants in the UK stayed in prison until the 2001 Act was repealed by Parliament in March 2005. Following their release, they were subject to restrictive regimes and were placed in immigration detention pending deportation to their countries of origin.

The applicants complained that their detention violated their rights under Article 3 of the Convention and that they were denied an effective remedy

8 A. and Others v. the United Kingdom—3455/05 [2009] ECHR 313 (19 February 2009).

for their complaints under Article 3, in violation of Article 13 of the Convention. They further complained that their detention was discriminatory and in breach of Article 14 of the Convention, while British nationals suspected of involvement with al-Qaeda were left free. The applicants also argued that the procedure for challenging their detention before the domestic courts did not comply with the requirements of Article 5(4).

Article 5 of the European Convention on Human Rights—Right to liberty and security

1. Everyone has the right to liberty and security of person. No one shall be deprived of his liberty save in the following cases and in accordance with a procedure prescribed by law:
(a) the lawful detention of a person after conviction by a competent court;
(b) the lawful arrest or detention of a person for noncompliance with the lawful order of a court or in order to secure the fulfilment of any obligation prescribed by law;
(c) the lawful arrest or detention of a person effected for the purpose of bringing him before the competent legal authority on reasonable suspicion of having committed an offence or when it is reasonably considered necessary to prevent his committing an offence or fleeing after having done so;
(d) the detention of a minor by lawful order for the purpose of educational supervision or his lawful detention for the purpose of bringing him before the competent legal authority;
(e) the lawful detention of persons for the prevention of the spreading of infectious diseases, of persons of unsound mind, alcoholics or drug addicts or vagrants;
(f) the lawful arrest or detention of a person to prevent his effecting an unauthorised entry into the country or of a person against whom action is being taken with a view to deportation or extradition.
2. Everyone who is arrested shall be informed promptly, in a language which he understands, of the reasons for his arrest and of any charge against him.
3. Everyone arrested or detained in accordance with the provisions of paragraph 1 (c) of this Article shall be brought promptly before a judge or other officer authorised by law to exercise judicial power and shall be entitled to trial within a reasonable time or to release pending trial. Release may be conditioned by guarantees to appear for trial.

> 4. Everyone who is deprived of his liberty by arrest or detention shall be entitled to take proceedings by which the lawfulness of his detention shall be decided speedily by a court and his release ordered if the detention is not lawful.
> 5. Everyone who has been the victim of arrest or detention in contravention of the provisions of this Article shall have an enforceable right to compensation.

1.2.2 Position of the Court

The case at hand was unusual in that the UK government admitted wrongdoing and challenged the decisions of its own high courts. However, the Court considered that this did not exclude the possibility of considering the applicants' complaint. The Court did not find a violation of Article 3 of the Convention but considered that a number of provisions of Article 5 of the Convention had been violated. The Court began its reasoning by noting that it was acutely aware of the difficulties that states faced in protecting their populations from terrorist violence. However, the Convention categorically prohibited torture and inhuman or degrading treatment or punishment (paragraph 126).

The Court considered that the uncertainty about their situation and the fear of indefinite detention must undoubtedly have caused the applicants great anxiety and distress, as would have been caused to virtually any detainee in their situation. Moreover, it is likely that the stress was sufficiently severe and prolonged to affect the mental health of some of the applicants (paragraph 130). However, the Court immediately made a reservation that it could not be said that the applicants had no prospect or hope of release. In particular, they were able to bring proceedings to challenge the legality of the detention scheme under the 2001 Act and were successful in having their case heard in the House of Lords. In these circumstances, the Court found no violation of Article 3, taken alone or in combination with Article 13 (paragraph 131).

The Court further noted that the requirement of procedural fairness under Article 5(4) of the Convention did not impose a single, unchanging standard which had to be applied regardless of the context, facts and circumstances (paragraph 203). Although a state of emergency was in force at the time of the applicants' detention, the applicants' trial was therefore required to be adversarial and to ensure 'equality of arms' between the parties (paragraph 204). In reality, some of the accused applicants were not made aware of the evidence establishing their links with terrorists, which prevented them from effectively challenging the charges against themselves (paragraphs 223–224). There has therefore been a violation of Article 5(4) in relation to these applicants. The Court also found violations of Articles 5(1) and (5). The Court justified the award of compensation on the basis that it had not been established that any of the applicants had participated or attempted to participate in any act of terrorist violence (paragraph 251).

1.3 *Amerkhanov v. Turkey (No. 16026/12)*[9]

1.3.1 Brief Overview of the Facts of the Case

On 5 June 2018, the European Court of Human Rights issued decisions in *Batyrkhairov v. Turkey* (complaint No. 69929/12)[10] and *Amerkhanov v. Turkey* (complaint No. 16026/12). Due to the similarity of these cases, we will consider only one of them. Both cases involved Kazakh citizens who were detained at the Kumkapi Alien Removal Centre in Turkey on suspicion of involvement in Islamic-inspired terrorist activities before being deported to Kazakhstan. Their requests for international protection were rejected by the Turkish authorities.

On 16 August 2011, the applicant was interviewed by the police, during which interview he expressed his fear of being subjected to a real risk of death or severe ill-treatment upon deportation to Kazakhstan. He claimed that he had already been targeted by the Kazakhstan authorities for his religious beliefs, and that he had been subjected to torture in the past. His lawyer, in turn, submitted evidence showing that the applicant was being sought by Kazakhstan for alleged involvement in 'hooliganism', a charge linked to his perceived religious extremism, and that an arrest warrant had been issued (paragraph 17).

Despite these serious concerns, the Turkish authorities proceeded with the deportation without fully assessing the risk the applicant faced in Kazakhstan. In a letter dated 27 May 2013 the applicant's lawyer, Mr. Yılmaz, claimed that the applicant was handed over to the Kazakhstani security forces upon his return to Kazakhstan and was subsequently detained in the Atyrau prison. The lawyer stated that he had no information, confirmed by any documents, regarding whether the applicant had been subjected to ill-treatment in Kazakhstan. The applicant complained of a violation by the Turkish authorities of Articles 3, 5 and 13 of the Convention.

1.3.2 Position of the Court

The Court found that the complaint had been satisfied in full and found a violation of all of these Articles. The Court noted that the applicant's deportation occurred before it had considered his complaint, so that the applic-

9 Amerkhanov v. Turkey—16026/12 [2018] ECHR 455 (5 June 2018).
10 Batyrkhairov v. Turkey—69929/12 [2018] ECHR 456 (5 June 2018).

ant was deprived of the opportunity to challenge his deportation in court (paragraph 56). In this case, the applicant, an asylum seeker, was deported to Kazakhstan, a non-Council of Europe State, in the absence of a legal procedure providing guarantees against unlawful deportation, and without a proper assessment of his application for asylum. Also, the deportation took place in the context of the applicant's fear of ill-treatment in Kazakhstan, for which no legal assessment was given. In this regard, there has been a violation of Article 3 of the Convention. The Court also noted that it had found a violation of Article 5(4) and (5) on account of the failure of the Turkish legal system to provide persons in the applicant's position with a remedy (paragraph 73).

The Court highlighted that, at the time, Kazakhstan was known for targeting individuals with Islamic beliefs in its efforts to combat terrorism, and there were numerous reports of the ill-treatment of such individuals by law enforcement. Given these circumstances, the Turkish authorities should have been aware of the potential danger the applicant faced, particularly as his religious views were framed as a justification for suspicion of terrorism (paragraphs 33–41). The failure of the Turkish authorities adequately to assess the risks of deportation, especially in the context of the applicant's alleged links to Islamic-inspired terrorism, led to a breach of his human rights under the Convention.

The Court also paid great attention to the conditions in which the applicant was detained before his deportation. In its view, the conditions of the applicant's detention at the Kumkapi Aliens Removal Centre—coupled with the possible anxiety caused by the uncertainty about when the detention would end—were sufficient to enable it to conclude that the conditions of his detention caused the applicant suffering beyond an unavoidable level suffering inherent in detention and reached the threshold of degrading treatment prohibited by Article 3 (paragraphs 87–88). The Court further found a violation of Article 13 of the Convention in the context of a violation of Article 3.

1.4 *Internationale Humanitäre Hilfsorganisation v. Germany (No. 11214/19)*[11]

1.4.1 Brief Overview of the Facts of the Case

The non-profit charitable organization, Internationale Humanitäre Hilfsorganisation e.V., was liquidated by the German authorities and its property confis-

11 Internationale Humanitäre Hilfsorganisation e.V. v. Germany—11214/19 [2023] ECHR 776 (10 October 2023).

cated for its pursuit of goals incompatible with the 'concept of international understanding'. This measure was based on the finding that the charity to which the plaintiff association gave almost half of its financial donations was associated with the terrorist organization, Hamas. The applicant association complained that its ban and the confiscation of its assets violated its right to freedom of association under Article 11 of the Convention.

1.4.2 Position of the Court

The Court did not find a violation of Article 11 of the Convention in this case. It was established that the applicant organisation did provide financial support to a banned Islamist association, which in turn redirected funds to Hamas. Thus, in the Court's view, the applicant must have been aware that he was in breach of the statutory prohibition (paragraph 70). The Court noted that the case concerned the fight against international terrorism in general, regardless of the actual threat to the respondent Contracting State (paragraph 75).

For this reason, despite the fact that the applicant association's stated purpose was 'to provide appropriate humanitarian assistance throughout the world in cases of natural disasters, wars and other catastrophes' (paragraph 5), the Court assessed the actions of the German Government as lawful and fair. Firstly, the applicant's financing of terrorist organisations was proven (paragraph 92). Secondly, the dissolution of the organisation occurred after a number of warnings from the authorities and attempts by its members to circumvent potential restrictions imposed on the organisation's activities. There was also the potential for the applicant to destroy evidence and transfer assets to proscribed organisations (paragraphs 100–101).

1.4.3 Intermediate Conclusions

In conclusion, the European Court of Human Rights has consistently reinforced the importance of safeguarding individual rights, particularly in the context of national security and anti-terrorism measures. The Court has been vigilant in ensuring that states do not adopt measures that unfairly target specific religious groups, particularly Muslims, under the guise of combating terrorism. In *Ahmet Arslan and Others v. Turkey*, the Court ruled that detaining individuals solely for wearing religious attire, such as Islamic clothing, was impermissible. This ruling reflects a critical stance against practices that discriminate against Muslims in the name of security, underscoring the necessity of providing substantial justification for any infringement on religious freedoms.

Further, the Court has established that the mere detention of individuals suspected of involvement in terrorism does not violate the European Convention, as long as it meets certain legal safeguards. For example, in *A. and Others v. the United Kingdom* (No. 3455/05), the Court emphasised the importance of providing detainees with access to legal assistance and ensuring that they were not subjected to torture or ill-treatment during their detention. This case establishes a key principle: while counterterrorism measures are necessary, they must respect fundamental human rights, including the rights to legal representation and a fair trial.

In *Amerkhanov v. Turkey* (No. 16026/12), the applicant was suspected of terrorism based on alleged links to radical Islam, a charge that raised significant concerns regarding his religious beliefs. The applicant feared being persecuted for these beliefs if deported to Kazakhstan, where he had already been targeted by the authorities for his religious views. The Court emphasised that the Turkish authorities should have carefully considered the real risk of ill-treatment he faced upon return, given its political and religious context. The decision stressed the importance of ensuring that individuals are not deported to countries where they face a credible threat of torture or persecution based on their religious convictions, even in the context of national security concerns.

Additionally, in *Internationale Humanitäre Hilfsorganisation v. Germany*, the Court addressed the issue of organisations that disguise terrorist activities as charitable actions. The ruling underscored the importance of states taking decisive action to prevent organisations that supported or engaged in terrorism from operating freely. However, it also emphasised that such measures had to be based on indisputable evidence, ensuring that states acted proportionally and within the boundaries of the law to protect national security and public order.

Collectively, these cases illustrate the European Court of Human Rights' firm stance on ensuring that counterterrorism measures respect fundamental human rights. The Court recognises the complexity of terrorism and the need for multifaceted responses, but it consistently upholds the principle that national security efforts must not come at the expense of individual freedoms, particularly that regarding religious rights. These rulings reinforce the importance of a balanced approach in addressing the threat of terrorism while protecting the rights and dignity of all individuals, regardless of their religious beliefs.

2 Violation of Muslims' Rights to Freedom of Speech and Expression as Part of Anti-terrorism Policy

2.1 *Sürek and Özdemir v. Turkey (No. 23927/94 and 24277/94)*[12]

2.1.1 Brief Overview of the Facts of the Case

The owner and editor-in-chief of a Turkish newspaper were convicted (with a fine for the owner and imprisonment and a fine for the editor-in-chief) of publishing an interview with a commander of the Kurdistan Workers' Party, which is banned in Turkey as an extremist group. The applicants filed a complaint with the ECtHR about a violation of their rights under Article 10 of the Convention.

2.1.2 Position of the Court

The Court found a violation of Article 10 of the Convention. It stated that since the applicants had been found guilty of publishing declarations of terrorist organisations and disseminating separatist propaganda through a magazine of which they were respectively the owner and the editor, the actions of the Turkish authorities had to be seen in the context of the role of the press in ensuring the proper functioning of political democracy (paragraph 58). The Court paid particular attention to the words used in the interview and the context in which it was published (paragraph 61).

In the Court's opinion, the published interviews as a whole could not be considered to incite violence or hatred, since they had informational content that allowed the public not only to gain an insight into the psychology of those who are the driving force behind the opposition to official policies in south-east Turkey, but also to evaluate what was happening within the conflict. At the same time, the Court demonstrated an understanding of the actions of the authorities, given the scale and severity of the situation around the Kurdish resistance.

However, the existence of a conflict, in the Court's opinion, could not be considered a sufficient basis for justifying such a radical interference with the applicants' right to freedom of expression. This followed from the absence of incitement to violence in the interviews published by the applicants and in the joint statement on this matter. Accordingly, the applicants' conviction and sentence were disproportionate to the aims pursued and were therefore not 'necessary in a democratic society'. It followed that in the specific circumstances of this case there had been a violation of Article 10 of the Convention.

12 Sürek and Özdemir v. Turkey—23927/94;24277/94 [1999] ECHR 50 (8 July 1999).

This decision caused controversy among the judges. The concurring opinion of Judges Pahl, Tulkens, Fischbach, Casadevall and Greve expressed the view that the majority's assessment of Article 10 against the respondent State placed too much weight on the words used in the publication and insufficient regard to the general context in which those words were used, and their likely impact.

Judge Bonello said that the presence of support for or the provocation of violence in a publication was not sufficient for a conviction by national courts in a democratic society. In his opinion, punishment by national authorities of those who encouraged violence would be justified in a democratic society only if the incitement was such as to create a 'clear and present danger'.

In turn, Judges Wildhaber, Kuris, Strazhnitskaya, Baki and Trai, in their joint dissenting opinion, took the position that freedom of expression under the Convention was not absolute, and there was no violation of Article 10 of the Convention. In their opinion, in a democratic society it was necessary to limit speech that constituted incitement to violence. However, in the context of the present proceedings, the judges considered that the victims' statements were relatively moderate. These views could not justify an interference with the applicants' right to freedom of expression. However, regarding the publication of the full interview of the rebel leader, the judges here considered it illegal, given the sensitivity of the political and security situation in south-east Turkey.

A similar opinion was expressed in a dissenting opinion by Judge Gelcuklu. He also did not see a violation of Article 10 of the Convention in this case. In his opinion, there were no compelling reasons to consider that intervention in this case was not necessary in a democratic society and, in particular, was not proportionate to the aim of preserving national security and public order.

2.2 *Gündüz v. Turkey (No. 35071/97a)*[13]

2.2.1 Brief Overview of the Facts of the Case

The applicant, a self-proclaimed member of an Islamic sect, criticised democracy and called for the introduction of Sharia law during a televised debate. A criminal case was brought against him on the ground that his speech incited violence and was based on religious intolerance. The applicant filed a complaint about a violation of his rights under Article 10 of the Convention.

2.2.2 Position of the Court

The Court found a violation of Article 10 of the Convention. First, it noted that the programme in question was dedicated to the applicant's sect, whose follow-

13 Gündüz v. Turkey—35071/97, § 51, ECHR 2003-XI (4 December 2003).

ers had attracted public attention. Accordingly, the topic concerned a matter of public interest, an area in which restrictions on freedom of expression must be strictly construed (paragraph 43). Although, in the Court's view, the applicant's remarks might have been offensive to some television viewers, it was important to bear in mind that they were made orally during a live television broadcast. This means that the applicant did not have the opportunity to reformulate, clarify or withdraw them before they were made public.

The Court separately stated that Sharia, which the applicant called for, and democracy were incompatible (paragraph 51). However, comparing this case with previous ones (for example, *Refah Partisi* (*Welfare Party*) *and others v. Turkey*), where similar conclusions about Sharia were reached, the Court noted that the expression of an opinion differs significantly from the programme the party seeks to implement. Thus, the very fact of defending Sharia law without calling for violence to establish it could not be considered 'incitement to hatred'. Moreover, the applicant's position was not hidden and was publicly known.

For this reason, the Court considered that the interference with the applicant's freedom of expression was not based on sufficient reasons for the purposes of Article 10 (paragraph 52). The punishment of two years' imprisonment was clearly disproportionate to the government's objectives. There has thus been a violation of Article 10 of the Convention.

Judge Thurman issued a dissenting opinion in which he disagreed with the Court's findings. The applicant had stated during a live broadcast of a very popular television programme that children born from common law marriages were bastards. This expression used what was a very offensive word in Turkish. For this reason, in Judge Thurman's opinion, the applicant's speech clearly contained hate speech which did not deserve protection.

2.3 *Sabuncu and Others v. Turkey (No. 23199/17)*[14]

2.3.1 Brief Review of the Actual Circumstances of the Case

The applicants were journalists and executives of the newspaper Cumhuriyet, a prominent opposition publication in Turkey. They were charged with various offences, including aiding a terrorist organisation, espionage and spreading terrorist propaganda, based on their journalistic activities and articles critical of the Turkish government.

The applicants argued that their prosecution and detention violated their right under Article 5 of the Convention to fair judicial proceedings and to free-

14 Sabuncu and Others v. Turkey—23199/17 [2020] ECHR 794 (10 November 2020).

dom of expression under Article 10 of the European Convention on Human Rights. They also referred to Article 18 of the Convention. They contended that they had been targeted for their journalistic work and that the charges against them were politically motivated.

2.3.2 Position of the Court

The Court found violations of Articles 5 and 10 of the Convention. It noted that although the measures against the applicants had been taken under judicial supervision, they were based on mere suspicion (paragraph 180). Due to a number of procedural irregularities, the Court concluded that there had been a violation of Article 5(1) of the Convention due to a lack of reasonable suspicion that all the applicants had committed a criminal offence.

In the Court's view, since the detention of the applicant journalists was not based on a reasonable suspicion that they had committed a crime, there was a violation of their right to liberty (paragraph 230). This followed from the fact that an unlawful measure of detention, insofar as it constituted an interference with one of the freedoms guaranteed by the Convention, could not in principle be considered as a restriction of that freedom provided for by national law. It followed that the interference with the applicants' rights and freedoms under Article 10 of the Convention could not be justified because it was not provided for by law. Accordingly, there had been a violation of Article 10 of the Convention.

Judge Yuksel, generally agreeing with the majority decision, made a number of his own comments on the case. Regarding Article 5(1), the Judge questioned the examination of journalistic content under Article 10 criteria. Instead, he advocated solely focusing on the attributability of acts to the applicants, assessing the reasonableness of suspicion under Article 5(1) (c). He disagreed with the necessity of delving into specific articles and messages, particularly citing reservations about paragraph 173 of the judgment due to pending applications related to the materials.

Concerning Article 10, the Court needed a separate examination of whether interference was 'prescribed by law', rather than automatically deeming there to have been a violation based on an Article 5 breach. Referring to previous case law, it argued that although the interference was lawful, it failed the necessity test. Therefore, while concurring with the violation of Article 10 by reason of disproportionate detention, he dissented on the approach to the necessity criterion.

Judge Kuris partially dissented in the case. He agreed with the majority's finding of a violation of Articles 5(1) and 10 of the Convention but disagreed with certain aspects of the reasoning.

1. Regarding Article 5(1), he questioned the examination of journalistic content under Article 10 criteria, advocating for a focus solely on attributability to the applicants.

2. Concerning Article 10, he emphasised the need for a separate examination of whether interference was 'prescribed by law', rather than automatically deeming there to have been a violation based on an Article 5 breach.

3. While concurring with the violation of Article 10 due to disproportionate detention, he dissented on the approach to the necessity criterion.

He partly dissented under Article 18 of the Convention. He disagreed with the majority's finding that there was no appearance of a violation of Article 18, asserting that there was evidence suggesting the possibility of political motives behind the applicants' detention.

2.3.3 Intermediate Conclusions

The European Court of Human Rights frequently addresses cases involving the promotion of religious extremist ideas, highlighting the challenge of balancing freedom of expression with the need to protect public order and safety. To counter radicalism and extremism effectively, it is essential to distinguish between speech that promotes extremist ideas and speech that directly or indirectly incites one to violence or harm. Propaganda, especially in the context of radical ideologies like Islamist extremism, involves the dissemination of ideas that justify violence or radical societal change. However, it is important to note that international law does not permit the criminalisation of all religious expression or extremist ideas but rather focuses on a restriction of speech that incites one to violence, hatred or discrimination.

The ECtHR's jurisprudence underlines the importance of this distinction. In cases such as *Sürek and Özdemir v. Turkey*, the Court examined the issue of journalistic freedom in the context of reporting on terrorism, ruling that interviewing terrorists does not, in itself, amount to supporting terrorism. The Court emphasised that journalistic activities should not be unjustly restricted based solely on the content of interviews or the subjects discussed, unless there is concrete evidence of support for violence or incitement. This reaffirms the Court's commitment to protecting the media's role in democratic societies, even when covering sensitive issues related to terrorism and extremism.

Similarly, in *Gündüz v. Turkey*, the Court ruled that the discussion of Sharia law on television, while potentially controversial, falls within the scope of protected speech. It recognised that public debate about religious ideologies and legal systems is vital to a democratic society. However, it also pointed out that any discussion that leads to hostility or incites violence could justify restrictions on freedom of speech. This decision further reinforces the principle that freedom of expression should not be curtailed unless speech directly incites harm.

In *Sabuncu and Others v. Turkey*, the Court addressed the prosecution of journalists accused of supporting terrorism simply for covering the activities of extremist groups. The Court ruled that the prosecution of journalists, without clear evidence of incitement or violence, was a violation of their right to freedom of expression. This case is particularly significant as it highlights the necessity of protecting journalistic freedom, even in cases involving national security concerns. It reiterates that freedom of expression is a fundamental right that should not be restricted unless there is a clear and direct link to violence or harm.

In line with the broader framework of international law, particularly the International Covenant on Civil and Political Rights (ICCPR), Article 19 protects the right to freedom of expression but acknowledges that it carries 'special duties and responsibilities'. Article 20(2) of the ICCPR requires States Parties to prohibit advocacy of national, racial or religious hatred that incites violence or discrimination. This aligns with the Court's decisions, which assert that restrictions on speech should target only advocacy that leads to violence or harm, not the expression of religious beliefs or extremist ideas *per se*.

The OSCE Office for Democratic Institutions and Human Rights (ODIHR) further emphasises that state authorities must carefully assess whether religious or extremist speech is truly inciting violence before imposing legal restrictions. Using tools such as the six-part test in the Rabat Plan of Action, States are encouraged to ensure that restrictions are narrowly focused on speech that clearly promotes violence or hatred. This nuanced approach ensures that States protect public order without unduly restricting religious or ideological expression.

In conclusion, the ECtHR's case law in *Sürek and Özdemir v. Turkey*, *Gündüz v. Turkey* and *Sabuncu and Others v. Turkey* highlights the importance of carefully distinguishing between speech that incites violence and speech that simply reports or promotes radical ideas. The Court consistently affirms that freedom of expression, particularly in relation to religious beliefs and political ideologies, must be safeguarded unless there is clear evidence of harm. These rulings align with international standards that require a proportional and context-specific approach to regulating speech, ensuring that restrictions are applied only when necessary to prevent incitement to violence or discrimination.

CHAPTER 5

Education and Schools

The European Court of Human Rights has seen an increasing number of cases related to the educational rights of Muslim students. These cases often involve complex intersections between various aspects of the European Convention on Human Rights, reflecting the multifaceted nature of educational rights within a religious context. The HUDOC database, a comprehensive repository of ECtHR cases, continues to expand, with cases addressing the nuanced challenges faced by Muslim students in public education systems across Europe.

Discrimination against Muslims in educational institutions is a significant concern, particularly when it affects children. Educational settings, as formative environments, should uphold values of equality and inclusivity, yet various forms of discrimination persist. One of the most prevalent forms of discrimination is the marginalisation or exclusion of Muslim students based on their religious practices, such as the wearing of the hijab or the observance of religious holidays. These practices, while integral to their identity, are sometimes viewed as incongruent with the norms of the broader society. Consequently, Muslim students may face prejudice, exclusion from certain activities, or even verbal and physical abuse from peers and educators alike.

The importance of addressing such discrimination is underlined by the fact that children are particularly vulnerable in these environments, and that the consequences can be long-lasting. The psychological and social effects of such discrimination, especially at a young age, can lead to feelings of alienation, low self-esteem, and an overall diminished sense of belonging. In many cases, this discrimination is compounded by a lack of understanding or sensitivity towards cultural and religious diversity among both educators and students, which can perpetuate stereotypes and further marginalise Muslim students.

As discussed earlier in the context of Article 14 of the ECHR, protection from discrimination, particularly on the grounds of religion, is paramount. The European Court of Human Rights has highlighted the need for States to provide 'weighty reasons' to justify any distinction based on religious affiliation, and this standard should be applied rigorously in the educational context. Discriminatory practices in schools not only violate the rights of Muslim students but also hinder the broader societal goals of integration and mutual respect for diversity. So any form of discrimination in educational settings, particularly towards children, requires urgent legal and social intervention to ensure that the victims' fundamental rights, as guaranteed under the Convention, are protected.

Furthermore, according to guidelines issued by the OSCE Office for Democratic Institutions and Human Rights (ODIHR), the Council of Europe and the United Nations Educational, Scientific and Cultural Organisation (UNESCO), manifestations of intolerance and discrimination in school settings can encompass a broad range of acts.[1] While these are most often committed by students, there are also instances where intolerance or discrimination is exhibited by teachers or school administrators. The worst forms of discrimination may constitute criminal offences and should be referred to the appropriate authorities. Such acts include threats, destruction or desecration of property, vandalism and violent attacks or assaults on individuals.

However, there are also manifestations of discrimination that, while they may be considered normal playground or school-yard behaviour, can be seriously detrimental to students' wellbeing. These include exclusion, verbal abuse, derogatory comments and name-calling. Even though these acts may seem less severe than violent offences, they can have long-term psychological and emotional consequences, especially for vulnerable groups like Muslim students. Addressing both overt and subtle forms of discrimination is crucial to ensure that educational environments are safe, inclusive and respectful for all students, regardless of their religious background.

A distinctive feature of cases concerning the educational rights of Muslim students is the ECtHR's approach to interpreting the right to education in conjunction with other rights and freedoms guaranteed by the European Convention on Human Rights. This holistic approach enables the Court to address the broader implications of educational policies and practices on the religious freedoms of Muslim students.

One of the primary issues in these cases is the right of Muslim students to wear religious clothing, such as the hijab, in educational settings. This matter intersects with broader debates on religious expression and secularism in public institutions. By focusing on this issue within the education sector, the ECtHR examines additional rights protected by the European Convention, highlighting the unique challenges faced by Muslim students.

While the right to wear religious clothing is a significant issue, other cases focus on religious education and instruction within public schools. These cases

1 *Guidelines for Educators on Countering Intolerance and Discrimination against Muslims: Addressing Islamophobia through Education* (2011), p. 18.

often involve the balance between respecting religious convictions and maintaining a secular educational environment.

The prohibition of discrimination is often considered alongside the right to education and religious freedom. The ECtHR scrutinises whether educational policies have a disproportionate impact on Muslim students, ensuring that States do not implement discriminatory practices under the guise of maintaining secularism.

Religion is increasingly recognised within public debate, a phenomenon described by Habermas as the post-secular. According to Habermas, citizen participation is possible via literary publics operating within the public sphere.[2] This perspective highlights the importance of public discourse and the role of religion in shaping societal values and policies.

The ECtHR's role in adjudicating on disputes related to the educational rights of Muslim students is crucial in ensuring that educational practices respect diverse religious convictions while upholding principles of secularism and equality. By considering multiple rights and freedoms in tandem, the Court seeks to balance individual rights with broader societal interests. The focus on the right to wear religious clothing in educational settings highlights the unique challenges faced by Muslim students, while cases on religious instruction and discrimination emphasise the need for inclusive and respectful educational policies.

This section examines European and Turkish cases separately to illustrate the differing contexts and challenges faced by Muslim students in these jurisdictions. In non-Islamic European countries, the main problem is the conflict between the established secular system of education and Islamic traditions. These cases often involve issues of religious attire, religious instruction and discrimination within a framework of strong secularism.

Conversely, the Turkish cases demonstrate the State's attempts simultaneously to support the constitutional principle of secularism and influence the religious sphere of society. Turkey, as a predominantly Muslim country with a strong secular tradition, faces unique challenges in balancing these principles. The ECtHR's jurisprudence in Turkish cases often reflects the tension between maintaining secular educational policies and accommodating religious practices.

---

2 See Habermas, Jürgen, *The Public Sphere: An Inquiry into a Category of Bourgeois Society*. Cambridge: Polity Press, 1989.

1 Public Education for Muslim Students in Jurisdictions with a Muslim Minority

1.1 *Dogru v. France (No. 27058/05)*[3]

1.1.1 Brief Overview of the Facts of the Case

The complainant in the case was a Muslim school-age girl. She had entered the government high school in the 1998–1999 school year. In January 1999, she repeatedly showed up for physical education and sports classes wearing a headscarf, which she refused to take off, despite the constant demands of the teacher, who explained that wearing headscarves in these classes was unacceptable. In February 1999, the school's student disciplinary committee decided to expel the applicant from school for systematically avoiding active participation in physical education and sports classes. The applicant lodged a complaint under Article 9 of the Convention.

1.1.2 Position of the Court

The Court found no violation of Article 9 of the Convention in this case. It concluded that the impugned interference had a sufficient legal basis in domestic law (paragraph 59). The Court also recalled that the State might restrict the freedom of expression of religion, for example, wearing the Muslim headscarf, if the exercise of this freedom was contrary to the purpose of protecting the rights and freedoms of others, public order and security (paragraph 64). By refusing to remove the headscarf, the applicant had exceeded the limits of the exercise of the right to express and manifest religious beliefs in an educational institution (paragraph 68).

At the same time, the Court noted that the wearing of religious signs was not in itself incompatible with the principle of the secular nature of school education, but became so in accordance with the conditions under which they were worn and the consequences that their wearing could have (paragraphs 70–75). In view of the above, the European Court considered that the punishment of permanent exclusion was not disproportionate and found that the applicant had the opportunity to continue her studies at a distance by online correspondence. Consequently, the applicant's religious beliefs were fully taken into account from the point of view of the protection of the rights and freedoms of others and public order. Consequently, there had been no violation of Article 9 of the Convention.

---

3 Dogru v. France—27058/05 [2008] ECHR 1579 (4 December 2008).

1.2 *Kervanci v. France (No. 31645/04)*[4]

1.2.1 Brief Overview of the Facts of the Case

This case is similar to the previous one. The disciplinary measure of expulsion from school for repeated refusal to remove the hijab during the hours of physical education does not breach Article 9 of the Convention or Article 2 of the first additional Protocol to the Convention.

1.3 *Osmanoglu and Kocabas v. Switzerland* (*No. 29086/12*)[5]

1.3.1 Brief Overview of the Facts of the Case

The case involved Turkish-Muslim parents residing in Switzerland who, for religious reasons, prevented their two daughters from attending mandatory swimming lessons at their public school. They argued that mixed-gender swimming violated the Islamic principle that women should remain separate from men. In 2010, the authorities ordered the parents to pay a fine of 1,400 Swiss francs (about 1,292 euros) because their daughters did not attend the required class. Under the applicable cantonal law, pupils could not be exempted until they reached puberty. According to the school, because the girls had not yet reached puberty, they were not eligible for an exemption from swimming lessons under Swiss law. In 2011, the parents began an action in a local court which rejected their claims, and in 2012 a Swiss federal court similarly rejected them, finding that the parents' right to freedom of religion had not been violated. The applicants applied to the ECtHR on the basis of a violation of Article 9 of the Convention.

1.3.2 Position of the Court

The ECtHR found no violation of Article 9 of the Convention. It pointed out that the school played a special role in the process of social integration, which became even more decisive when it came to children of foreign origin. Given the importance of compulsory education for children's development, exemption from certain lessons was justified only in very exceptional circumstances, under clearly defined conditions and taking into account equal treatment of all religious groups (paragraph 96).

Speaking about swimming in particular, the Court noted that the child's interest in attending such classes lay not simply in learning to swim and exercise, but, above all, in participating in this activity together with all other students, without exception, based on the child's background or parents and religious or philosophical beliefs (paragraphs 98, 100).

---

4 Kervanci v. France—31645/04 ECtHR (4 March 2009).

5 Osmanoglu and Kocabas v. Switzerland—29086/12 [2017] ECHR 14 (10 January 2017).

The Court also held that in the present case the authorities had offered the applicants very flexible terms in which their daughters were allowed, among other concessions, to wear burkinis to swimming lessons and could undress and shower in the absence of boys. These measures were intended to reduce the perceived impact of children's participation in mixed swimming classes on their parents' religious beliefs (paragraph 101).

Having regard to the above considerations, the Court considered that, by giving priority to the children's obligation to follow the full school curriculum and their successful integration over the applicants' private interests in obtaining an exemption from mixed swimming lessons for their daughters on religious grounds, the domestic authorities had not exceeded the significant margin of appreciation afforded to them in present case, which concerned compulsory education.

1.3.3 Intermediate Conclusions

The European Court of Human Rights has extensively examined the rights of Muslims in the context of public education for Islamic children in jurisdictions with an Islamic minority. These cases primarily involve issues related to the wearing of Islamic clothing by minor children in educational institutions in non-Muslim countries. The Court's decisions emphasise the balance between individual religious freedoms and the principles of secularism upheld by the host countries.

One prominent case is *Dogru v. France*, where the ECtHR upheld the French government's decision to prohibit the wearing of headscarves by students in public schools. The Court emphasised that in a secular society restrictions on wearing religious clothing are permissible if they are aimed at preserving public order and the rights and freedoms of others. Similarly, in *Kervanci v. France*, the Court reinforced this stance, reiterating that secularism is a legitimate aim that justifies certain limitations on the expression of religious beliefs in public institutions, particularly schools.

The ECtHR's rulings in these cases highlight the importance of secularism in public education. The Court has consistently held that States have a margin of appreciation in determining the extent to which religious symbols can be displayed in public spaces, including schools. This principle is particularly relevant in countries like France, where secularism (*laïcité*) is a fundamental aspect of the national identity and legal framework.

Another significant case is *Osmanoglu and Kocabas v. Switzerland*, where the issue was whether parents could refuse to allow their daughters to participate in mixed-gender swimming lessons due to their religious beliefs. The Court ruled that the State has the right to require full participation in the school curriculum, including activities that may conflict with religious views, such as swimming lessons. The ECtHR found that such requirements are justified in the interest of social integration and gender equality, which are fundamental values in a democratic society.

The Court's position in these cases underlines that, while religious freedoms are protected under the European Convention on Human Rights, they are not absolute. The ECtHR has consistently ruled that limitations can be imposed, especially in the context of public education, to uphold the principles of secularism and to ensure that all students, regardless of their religious background, receive a comprehensive education.

The ECtHR also acknowledges that educational institutions can make certain adjustments to respect religious practices. However, as seen in *Osmanoglu and Kocabas v. Switzerland*, these do not extend to exempting students from fundamental aspects of the curriculum. The Court noted that the educational institution in this case made concessions by allowing students to wear suitable clothing for swimming lessons that aligned with their religious beliefs. This approach reflects the Court's effort to strike a balance between respecting religious diversity and maintaining a unified educational system.

In these rulings the ECtHR has consistently emphasised the importance of integrating children from Muslim families into the secular fabric of the host society. The Court argues that such integration is essential for fostering social cohesion and ensuring that all children have equal opportunities to participate fully in the life of the community. This perspective is rooted in the belief that exposure to a secular and inclusive educational environment helps to promote mutual understanding and respect among individuals of different religious and cultural backgrounds.

2 Public Education for Muslim Students in Jurisdictions with a Muslim Majority

2.1 *Leyla Shahin v. Turkey (No. 44774/98)*[6]

2.1.1 Brief Overview of the Facts of the Case

This case has become a precedent in the practice of the ECtHR. It is on the basis of this case that all cases related to the wearing of religious clothing by Muslims in educational institutions are resolved.

6 Leyla Shahin v. Turkey—44774/98 [2004] ECHR 299 (29 June 2004).

A medical student at Istanbul University had been disciplined for refusing to stop wearing the Muslim hijab. The applicant considered that these prohibitions violated Article 9 of the Convention.

2.1.2 Position of the Court

The Court did not find a violation of the Convention. It began by noting the permissibility of restrictions on the wearing of the Islamic headscarf in a democratic society and a university in particular (paragraph 98–99). In relation to the case itself, the Court pointed out that the interference was based in particular on two principles—secularism and equality (including gender)—which reinforced and complemented each other (paragraph 104). It noted the conformity of these principles with the Convention (paragraphs 106–107).

The Court added that when considering the Islamic hijab in the Turkish context, it was necessary to take into account the political and cultural impact that the wearing of such a symbol which, presented or perceived as an obligatory religious obligation, might have on those who chose not to wear it (paragraph 108).

The Court made particular reference to the fact that the resolution adopted by Istanbul University prohibiting the wearing of religious clothing on university premises treated all forms of clothing symbolising or expressing religion or belief on an equal footing, prohibiting them from being on university premises (paragraph 111).

In light of the above and taking into account in particular the margin of appreciation afforded to the Contracting States, the Court concluded that the Istanbul University regulations establishing restrictions on the wearing of Islamic headscarves and the measures taken to implement them were justified. in principle and proportionate to the aims pursued and could therefore be regarded as 'necessary in a democratic society'. Consequently, there was no violation of Article 9 of the Convention.

2.2 *Kose and Others v. Turkey (No. 26625/02)*[7]

2.2.1 Brief Overview of the Facts of the Case

Students at a religious public school challenged a ban on admitting people wearing the Islamic headscarf to school. The ban allowed an exception: covering the head was allowed in only one case—during the study of the Qur'an. The applicants considered that this violated the first sentence of Article 2 of Protocol No. 1 to the Convention and Article 9 of the Convention, since the ban

7 Köse and Others v. Turkey—26625/02 [2006] ECHR 1175 (24 January 2006).

on wearing the hijab in secondary schools deprived them of the right to education and the right of access to school.

2.2.2 Position of the Court

The Court found no violations in this case. It noted that the right to education was not absolute and might be subject to restrictions. This was implicitly permitted because 'the right of access by its nature requires regulation by the state'. In the present case, the Court noted that the measures taken against the pupils were clearly foreseeable because the pupils had undertaken to comply with dress codes upon enrolment. As in the previous case, *Leyla Şahin v. Turkey*, the Court reiterated that allowing students to wear the Islamic hijab was incompatible with the principle of secularism.

The Court also noted that permission for girls to wear the hijab during Qur'an lessons meant that there was no strict prohibition on wearing it. There was only a set of rules allowing girls to wear a headscarf during Qur'an lessons. Moreover, the ban on access to the school was introduced only after students, in violation of the rules, refused to remove their hijab on school grounds. Thus, these measures were taken as a last resort to restore calm in schools where protest-related unrest was spreading after attempts at reconciliation by school authorities failed. Consequently, there was no violation of Article 2 of Protocol No. 1 to the Convention.

Regarding the violation of Article 9 of the Convention, the Court responded that the obligation imposed on pupils to wear a school uniform and not to cover their heads in school was a general rule applicable to all pupils, regardless of their religious beliefs. Consequently, in the light of the considerations set out above in relation to Article 2 of Protocol No. 1, even assuming that the applicants' right to manifest their religion was violated, the Court found no indication of a violation of Article 9.

2.3 *Hasan and Eylem Zengin v. Turkey (No. 1448/04)*[8]

2.3.1 Brief Overview of the Facts of the Case

The applicant and his daughter, belonging to the Alevi religious community, appealed to the ECtHR on the basis that his daughter's school prohibited her from refusing religious education lessons. The applicants argued, in particular, that the manner in which religious culture and ethics were taught in Turkey violated Ms Zengin's right to freedom of religion and the right of her parents to provide her with an education that was in accordance with their reli-

8 Hasan and Eylem Zengin v. Turkey—1448/04 [2007] ECHR 787 (9 October 2007).

gious beliefs, guaranteed by Article 2 of the Protocol. No. 1 (right to education) and Article 9 (freedom of thought, conscience and religion). The applicants argued that the course syllabus was not objective because it did not include any detailed information about other religions and was taught from a religious perspective that privileged the Sunni interpretation of Islamic faith and traditions.

2.3.2 Position of the Court

The Court found that there was a violation of Article 2 of Protocol No. 1 (right to education) of the European Convention on Human Rights. Thus, it began by noting that the right to education also implied the right of parents to respect for their religious and philosophical beliefs (paragraphs 48–50). In addition, the Court stated that the State, in discharging its functions in relation to education and teaching, had to ensure that information or knowledge included in the curriculum was imparted in an objective, critical and pluralistic manner that enabled students to develop critical thinking in relation to religion (paragraph 52).

The Court concluded that the applicant's primary school curriculum did indeed give greater priority to knowledge of Islam than to knowledge of other religions and philosophies. In the Court's view, this could not in itself be regarded as a departure from the principles of pluralism and objectivity, which would amount to indoctrination, given the fact that, despite the secular nature of the State, Islam was the main religion professed in Turkey (paragraph 63). However, in 'religious culture and morals' classes, the religious diversity that prevails in Turkish society is not taken into account. In particular, students do not obtain knowledge of the confessional or ritual features of the Alevi faith, although the proportion of the Turkish population belonging to it is very large (paragraph 67).

However, in the Court's view, parents of pupils could legitimately expect that the subject would be taught in a manner that met the criteria of objectivity and pluralism and with respect for their religious or philosophical beliefs. In light of this, the Court concluded that teaching religious culture did not meet the requirements of objectivity and pluralism, and therefore the restriction on a refusal to study this subject violated Article 2 of Protocol No. 1 (the right to education) to the European Convention on Human Rights (paragraph 76).

In conclusion, the Court noted that it made no sense to consider a violation of Article 9 of the Convention after the proceedings had been concluded.

2.4 *Mansur Yalcin and others v. Turkey* (*No. 21163/11*)[9]

2.4.1 Brief Overview of the Facts of the Case

As in the previous case, the applicants, who were Alevi, complained that refusal to exempt them from the religious education course represented a violation of the right of parents to raise their children in accordance with their religious beliefs.

2.4.2 Position of the Court

The Court again found a violation of Article 2 of Protocol No. 1 to the Convention. It noted that following the decision in *Hasan and Eylem Zengin v. Turkey* some changes had been made to the religious culture and ethics curriculum. First, these changes were facilitated by the provision of information about the various religions existing in Turkey, including the Alevi faith. However, these changes did not entail a real revision of the key components of the curriculum, which focused primarily on the knowledge of Sunni Islam as practised and interpreted by the majority of the Turkish population (paragraph 68). Based on this, the Court ruled that the key issue in the dispute between the parties was the content of the teaching of Islam in compulsory classes.

While refusing to examine the question of the correct interpretation of Islam in the school curriculum, the Court expressed the view that the State, as the ultimate guarantor of pluralism, including religious pluralism, in a democratic society, has an obligation to remain neutral and impartial (paragraph 70). Since the Turkish system offers exemption from classes in religious culture and ethics to only two categories of students of Turkish nationality, namely those whose parents are followers of the Christian or Jewish faith, this inevitably implies that teaching this subject is likely to result in these groups of pupils facing conflicts between the religious instruction provided by the school and their parents' religious or philosophical beliefs (paragraphs 76–77). For this reason, the Court concluded that the Turkish education system did not offer suitable options for the children of parents who had religious or philosophical beliefs other than those of Sunni Islam. Thus, in the present case there had been a violation of Article 2 of Protocol No. 1.

2.4.3 Intermediate Conclusions

The European Court of Human Rights' case law on public education in Muslim-majority countries mainly covers issues such as the ban on wearing Islamic religious dress, the nature of religious education and the problems faced by

9 Mansur Yalcin and others v. Turkey—21163/11 [2014] ECHR 938 (16 September 2014).

religious minorities such as the Alevi in Turkey. The Court's decisions highlight the delicate balance between maintaining secularism and respecting religious freedoms.

One of the landmark cases in this domain is *Leyla Şahin v. Turkey*. Here, the ECtHR upheld the ban on wearing the hijab in Turkish universities, emphasising that such a prohibition does not violate the European Convention on Human Rights. The Court reasoned that the ban was necessary to preserve the principles of secularism and equality in public institutions. This decision underlines the Court's stance that the primacy of secularism in democratic societies permits limitations on religious expression in public spaces in order to maintain state neutrality and equality.

Similarly, in *Köse and Others v. Turkey*, the ECtHR reiterated this position, asserting that even in religiously affiliated public schools students had to adhere to constitutional requirements of secularism. The Court held that upon entering a public educational institution students implicitly accepted its rules, including those governing dress codes. Therefore, claims of religious rights violations in this context were not sustainable if the institution's regulations were designed to uphold secular principles.

The Court's decisions consistently emphasise the importance of secularism in public education. The rulings in *Leyla Şahin v. Turkey* and *Köse and Others v. Turkey* articulate the view that secularism is essential for maintaining equality and neutrality in public institutions. By limiting religious expression, such as the wearing of Islamic clothing, in these settings, the Court aims to prevent any form of religious influence or discrimination, ensuring that all students are treated equally regardless of their religious background.

The issue of religious education for children from Islamic families, particularly from those of religious minorities like the Alevi, has also been a significant concern. In *Hasan and Eylem Zengin v. Turkey*, the ECtHR found that the Turkish educational curriculum, which emphasised Sunni Islam, did not comply with the requirements of the European Convention. The Court held that such an emphasis failed to respect the principles of state neutrality and pluralism in religious matters. This ruling highlights the necessity for educational programmes to be inclusive and representative of the diverse religious landscape, ensuring that minority beliefs are not marginalised.

Furthermore, in *Mansur Yalçin and Others v. Turkey*, the Court determined that the introduction of religious content reflecting only the dominant religious perspectives in the school curriculum, without adequate inclusion of other beliefs, was inconsistent with the Convention's principles. This case reaffirmed the importance of educational pluralism and the need for the curriculum to reflect the diverse religious makeup of the student body.

CHAPTER 6

Violation of the Electoral and Labour Rights of Muslims

Over the past few decades, Muslim immigrant communities in Europe have garnered significant attention from researchers. While the primary focus in the 1980s and 1990s was on labour migration and the formation of immigrant communities, contemporary studies have shifted towards examining the integration of immigrants into host societies and their impact on the internal dynamics of European countries. A critical aspect of these studies is the realisation of economic and political rights by Muslims, which serves as a particularly illustrative example for understanding broader social and political trends.[1]

The right to participate in free and fair elections is a cornerstone of democratic societies, and this right extends to all citizens, including Muslim immigrants and their descendants. However, Muslim communities often face unique challenges in exercising their electoral rights. These challenges include societal prejudice, structural barriers and political underrepresentation.

Electoral rights for Muslims relate primarily to elections to bodies of religious self-government, such as mosque councils or Islamic cultural centres. These institutions play a crucial role in the religious and social life of Muslim communities; and ensuring fair electoral processes within these bodies is essential for maintaining their legitimacy and effectiveness. Additionally, electoral rights can also pertain to ordinary voting in national and local elections, as well as running for public office. Muslim communities may face particular challenges in these areas due to discrimination and social prejudice. One significant political issue for Muslims is the high degree of dependence on the international situation and policies of other States. Internal trends within these communities are often heavily influenced by global events and foreign policies.

The labour rights of Muslims are also a significant concern. Discrimination in the workplace, barriers to employment and issues related to religious expression at work are prevalent challenges that Muslim employees face. The

1 Joppke, Christian, and Torpey, John, *Legal Integration of Islam: A Transatlantic Comparison.* (Cambridge MA: Harvard University Press, 2013), p. 47.

European legal framework, including various anti-discrimination laws, aims to protect the rights of all workers. However, the practical implementation of these laws can be inconsistent.

Muslim workers often face discrimination based on their religious beliefs and practices. This can include issues such as dress codes that prohibit religious attire, such as the hijab, and workplace policies that do not accommodate religious practices, such as prayer times. These issues are particularly pronounced in public institutions, where the principle of secularism is often invoked to justify restrictive measures.

Labour rights are also closely tied to the structure of religious associations, which are often subject to state control.[2] Many governments implement religious policies aimed at suppressing fundamentalism and depoliticising the religious sphere as much as possible. This can lead to conflicts when policies intended to ensure secularism inadvertently result in discrimination against Muslim employees. Employers, especially in the public sector, are tasked with maintaining neutrality while respecting individual religious freedoms. This balance can be delicate and challenging to navigate.

In many European countries, the balance between upholding secularism in public institutions and accommodating religious diversity is delicate. Employers, especially in public sectors, are tasked with maintaining neutrality while respecting individual religious freedoms. This often leads to conflicts where policies intended to ensure secularism inadvertently result in discrimination against Muslim employees.

The ECtHR not only seeks to integrate Muslims into the European legal system but also aims to extend to them the general legal regime, which includes both rights and restrictions. According to the logic of the European Convention, these restrictions can prevail over individual religious beliefs when necessary to maintain public order and protect the rights of others.

The ECtHR's approach often involves a delicate balancing act between upholding religious freedoms and ensuring that these freedoms do not infringe upon the rights and security of the wider community. This balancing act is particularly evident in cases involving the electoral and labour rights of Muslims, where the Court must consider both the right to religious expression and the need to maintain a secular and neutral public sphere.

2 Di Stasio, Valentina, et al., 'Muslim by Default or Religious Discrimination? Results from a Cross-National Field Experiment on Hiring Discrimination', *Journal of Ethnic and Migration Studies* 47.6 (2021), pp. 1305–1326.

1 Violation of Muslim Electoral Rights

1.1 *Agga v. Greece (No. 50776/99 and 52912/99)*[3]

1.1.1 Brief Overview of the Facts of the Case

The case concerned the same circumstances as *Serif v. Greece* (No. 38178/97). The applicant contested his removal from the post of one of the muftis of the Greek region of Thrace and his subsequent criminal prosecution for his refusal to resign. Like the suspended Mufti in *Serif v. Greece*, the applicant was accused of usurping the functions of a minister of a 'known religion'. The Greek Court of Cassation, considering that there might be unrest in the applicant's home town, ruled that the proceedings should take place in another town. In his complaint to the ECtHR, the applicant alleged a violation of Articles 9 and 10 of the Convention.

1.1.2 Position of the Court

The Court held that there had been a violation of only Article 9 of the Convention. It recalled that freedom of thought, conscience and religion was one of the foundations of a 'democratic society' within the meaning of the Convention. On this depended the pluralism inherent in a democratic society, won at great cost over the centuries (paragraph 56).

Due to the fact that the domestic courts did not mention in their decisions any specific actions of the applicant intended to give rise to legal consequences associated with the activities of the mufti, indicating only that he had published messages with religious content and signed them as the Mufti of Xanthi, the Court considered that this was incompatible with the requirements of religious pluralism in a democratic society (paragraph 58). In essence, the charge was based on the fact that the applicant had simply presented himself as the religious leader of a group that willingly followed him.

In the light of all the above, the Court concluded that there had been a violation of Article 9 of the Convention.

1.2 *Seyidzade v. Azerbaijan (No. 37700/05)*[4]

1.2.1 Brief Overview of the Facts of the Case

The applicant was refused registration as a candidate for the parliamentary elections on the grounds that he carried out religious activities. These activities consisted of teaching at a religious educational institution. However, at the

3 Agga v. Greece (No. 3)—32186/02 [2006] ECHR 784 (13 July 2006).
4 Seyidzade v. Azerbaijan—37700/05 [2009] ECHR 1983 (3 December 2009).

time of registration, the applicant had left all the positions he had held at the educational institution. In his view, refusal to register amounted to a violation of Article 3 of Protocol No. 1 to the ECtHR.

Article 3 of Protocol No. 1 to the European Convention on Human Rights—Right to free elections

The High Contracting Parties undertake to hold free elections at reasonable intervals by secret ballot, under conditions which will ensure the free expression of the opinion of the people in the choice of the legislature.

1.2.2 Position of the Court

The Court sided with the applicant and found a violation of Article 3 of Protocol No. 1 to the ECtHR. It stated that the main issue in the present case was the alleged unpredictability and arbitrariness of the measure taken (paragraph 32). Thus, the Electoral Code did not prevent clergy from standing for election and being elected but simply required that they cease their religious activities if elected to parliament (paragraph 34). The Court noted that in this particular case, by deciding to reject the applicant's request to register as a candidate on the basis of the relevant statutory provisions, the domestic authorities had implicitly held that those provisions limited the very right of 'clerics' to stand as candidates. Therefore, for the purposes of the present case, the Court continued its further analysis on the basis of the above approach adopted by the Azerbaijani authorities.

First, the Court found that the relevant domestic law was not sufficiently clear and precise to prevent arbitrary decisions by electoral authorities in determining whether a particular individual fell into a category whose rights were limited. In particular, the legislation did not in any way clarify the concept of 'religious activity' (paragraph 36). The domestic courts in the present case also did not provide any definitions or explanations (paragraph 38).

In these circumstances, the Court held that the domestic law providing for the alleged restriction was not foreseeable as to its consequences and left considerable room for speculation as to the definition of the categories of persons affected by it. It followed that there had been a violation of Article 3 of Protocol No. 1 to the Convention.

Some of the judges considered it necessary to add comments on the present case. In a concurring opinion, Justices Malinverni, Vayich and Kovler expressed the view that a legislative act, whatever its nature and whatever area it regulated and purported to regulate, was of necessity an abstract and general instrument. Therefore, they did not agree with the decision of the Court in terms of indicating the vagueness of the wording of the Azerbaijani electoral legislation. From the Judges' point of view, the violation consisted of a refusal to register due to the fact that the applicant did not carry out religious activities. It is therefore not the legislation as such that ought to be criticised in the present case, but the way in which it was applied by the courts.

1.3 *Medžlis Islamske Zajednice Brčko and Others v. Bosnia and Herzegovina (No. 17224/11)*[5]

1.3.1 Brief Overview of the Facts of the Case

The applicants were four Bosnian Islamic religious organisations that were fined for causing non-pecuniary damage to the candidate for the post of director of a public radio station, accusing her of Islamophobia. The allegations were made by the applicants to local authorities with the indication that the applicants reserved the right to contact the media if their complaint was not addressed. However, they subsequently failed to verify the veracity of these accusations. The applicant organisations were fined for this. In their complaint to the ECtHR they alleged a violation of Articles 8 and 10 of the Convention.

1.3.2 Position of the Court

The Court did not find a violation of the Convention. It found that the applicants' letter to the local authorities contained factual allegations and value judgments about the candidate's alleged misconduct. In this regard, it was necessary to understand how admissible these allegations were (paragraph 32). Although the applicants did not use offensive, harsh or intemperate language in their letter, they conveyed the information without making reasonable efforts to verify its accuracy. However, the applicants subsequently did not withdraw their accusations (paragraph 34).

The Court, having regard to the general circumstances of the present case, held that the domestic courts' decision struck a fair balance between the competing interests of the plaintiff and those of the applicants. Accordingly, there was no violation of the Articles of the Convention in question.

Some of the Judges disagreed with this decision. According to Judges Nikolaou, Tsotsoriya and Vehabovic, there has been a violation of Article 10 of the Convention. The Judges took the position that the applicants were not responsible for the distribution of the letter complained of. Thus, they had communicated it to the competent authorities, while the communication was both private and confidential and was addressed to persons who had a direct insti-

5 Medžlis Islamske Zajednice Brčko and Others v. Bosnia and Herzegovina—17224/11 [2015] ECHR 873 (13 October 2015).

tutional interest in the matter and were thus entitled to receive it. The fact that the applicants reserved the right to contact the media if the authorities failed to take action did not detract from this argument, since in reality there was no appeal to the media.

The Judges noted that the essence of the matter was that the authorities were obliged to pay attention to the said 'unofficial information' and, if it turned out to be substantiated, to take appropriate measures. It was clear that the applicants relied on the authorities to investigate and assess the various allegations. Therefore, the measures taken against the applicants clearly violated their right to freedom of expression in accordance with Article 10 of the Convention.

1.3.3 Intermediate Conclusions

The European Court of Human Rights has played a significant role in addressing the violation of electoral rights of Muslims, embracing active and passive suffrage as well as the public interest in candidacies for public office. The ECtHR's decisions in these cases illustrate its commitment to ensuring that restrictions on the political rights of Muslims comply with the European Convention on Human Rights. This text examines notable cases and their implications on the voting rights of Muslims.

In *Agga v. Greece*, the ECtHR dealt with the issue of restricting the freedom of a religious figure, namely the Mufti, for organising and participating in unsanctioned elections for the post of head of a religious community. The Greek authorities had imposed sanctions on Agga, arguing that his actions conflicted with the current legal regulations and could potentially cause unrest. However, the ECtHR found that such restrictions were unacceptable, particularly in the absence of any legal consequences of his participation. The Court emphasised that the prevention of unrest was not a sufficient justification for curbing the freedom of religious figures to engage in the organisation of and participation in elections within their religious community. This ruling emphasises the importance of protecting religious leaders' political rights, even when they challenge existing legal frameworks.

The *Seyidzade v. Azerbaijan* case highlights the issue of a former clergyman being denied the right to stand for election. The Azerbaijani authorities had refused Seyidzade's candidacy based on vague legal wording and a restrictive interpretation of the law by national courts. The ECtHR ruled that such a refusal was contrary to the European Convention. The Court's decision stressed that the issue was not merely the refusal itself, but the justification provided by the authorities which lacked clarity and precision. This case exemplifies the ECtHR's stance that electoral laws must be clear and unambiguous to prevent arbitrary interpretations that could unjustly restrict individuals' political rights.

The ECtHR's jurisprudence on the voting rights of Muslims highlights several key principles. Firstly, the restriction of political rights based on vague legal provisions or arbitrary interpretations is unacceptable. Electoral laws must be clear and precise to prevent unjust limitations on individuals' rights to stand for election. Secondly, the participation of religious figures in unsanctioned elections within their communities should not be restricted without substantial and justified reasons, particularly when such participation does not lead to legal consequences or public disorder.

In *Medžlis Islamske Zajednice Brčko and Others v. Bosnia and Herzegovina*, the ECtHR addressed the responsibilities of individuals and organisations in making complaints about candidates for public positions. The applicants had sent letters to government authorities alleging that a candidate for a public position was Islamophobic. These letters were based on information from third-party publications. The authorities subsequently held the complainants liable for misinformation and slander.

The ECtHR noted that while the State has the right to hold dishonest complainants accountable, this responsibility must be balanced with its duty thoroughly to verify information received from citizens and organisations. The Court emphasised that liability for misinformation did not exclude the responsibility of the State to ensure the accuracy of the information before acting upon it. This case underscores the need for a careful and balanced approach in handling complaints about candidates for public office, ensuring that both the integrity of the electoral process and the rights of individuals and organisations are protected.

In summary, the ECtHR's decisions demonstrate a commitment to protecting the political rights of Muslims while ensuring that restrictions are justified, clear and not arbitrary. The Court's rulings reinforce the importance of transparency, fairness and accountability in electoral processes, thereby upholding the principles of democracy and human rights enshrined in the European Convention on Human Rights.

2 Discrimination against Muslims in the Workplace

2.1 *Kalaç v. Turkey (No. 20704/92)*[6]

2.1.1 Brief Overview of the Facts of the Case

The applicant argued that his forced resignation from his position as a military Judge Advocate in the Air Force violated his freedom of religion (Article 9 of the

6 Kalac v. Turkey—20704/92 [1997] ECHR 37 (1 July 1997).

Convention), asserting that it was based on his religious beliefs and practices. He was compelled to retire due to what was described as 'illegal fundamentalist views' (paragraph 8). As a practising Muslim, the applicant consistently prayed five times a day and observed the Ramadan fast, adhering strictly to his faith. The applicant also noted that his religious practices had not interfered with his professional duties and responsibilities. He further disagreed with the decision of his superiors, claiming that the reasons behind his dismissal from the service were unjust and discriminatory, as they were based on his personal religious convictions rather than on any professional shortcomings. Despite his service record, which he contended was exemplary, the applicant maintained that his religious beliefs were wrongfully used as grounds for his forced resignation, infringing his rights to practise his religion freely without fear of retaliation.

2.1.2 Position of the Court

The Court found no violations of Article 9 of the Convention. It began by reiterating its position that Article 9 of the Convention does not protect every act motivated or inspired by religion or belief. Moreover, by exercising his freedom to manifest his religion, a person may have to take into account his particular situation (paragraph 27). According to the Court, by choosing a military career the applicant had voluntarily accepted a system of military discipline which, by its very nature, implied the possibility of imposing restrictions on certain rights and freedoms of military personnel which were beyond their control (paragraph 28). At the same time, the applicant was allowed to perform some religious rituals (paragraph 29).

On this basis, the Court concluded that the applicant's forced retirement did not constitute an interference with the right guaranteed by Article 9, since it was not caused by the applicant's practice of his religion.

2.2 *Hasan and Chaush v. Bulgaria (No. 30985/96)*[7]

2.2.1 Brief Overview of the Facts of the Case

The case relates to the same circumstances as *Supreme Holy Council of the Muslim Community v. Bulgaria* (No. 39023/97). The events of this case took place several years earlier than that one; the applicants here were representatives of the Bulgarian Muslim community, who subsequently, with the help of the democratic party that came to power, removed the leader of the opposing community in 1997.

---

7 Hasan and Chaush v. Bulgaria—30985/96 [2000] ECHR 511 (26 October 2000).

In the present case, the first applicant had held the position of Chief Mufti of Bulgarian Muslims until 1995. He lost his position after the new government decided to register another leader of a rival faction. The first applicant and his employees were then forcibly evicted from their offices in Sofia by private security guards led by the newly registered leaders. Prosecutors did nothing to help him, and his appeal to the Supreme Court against the authorities' decision to recognise the rival leader was rejected.

The applicants complained under Articles 9 (freedom of religion) and 11 (freedom of assembly and association) of the European Convention on Human Rights that there had been an unlawful and arbitrary interference with their religious freedoms and the rights of believers and religious communities, in particular to manage their affairs and choose their leaders. They also lodged complaints under Articles 6 (right to a fair trial) and 13 (right to an effective remedy).

2.2.2 Position of the Court

Just as in *Supreme Holy Council of the Muslim Community v. Bulgaria* the Court found a violation of Article 9 of the Convention. It noted that in the present case the relevant law did not provide for any substantive criteria on the basis of which the Council of Ministers and the Directorate of Religious Denominations register religious denominations and changes in their leadership in a situation of internal disagreements and conflicting claims to legitimacy. Moreover, there are no procedural safeguards, such as adversarial proceedings before an independent body, against the arbitrary exercise of powers vested in the executive (paragraph 85). The Court also indicated that the change in community leadership in 1995, as in 1992 and 1997, occurred shortly after the change of government. There has thus been a violation of Article 9 of the Convention.

The Court also found a violation of Article 13 of the Convention. In its opinion, the applicant sought a remedy for interference in the internal organisation of a religious community by challenging his removal in the Supreme Court. However, the Supreme Court refused to examine the substantive issues, holding that the Council of Ministers had full discretion to register or not the charter and leadership of a religious denomination, and ruled only on the formal issue of whether the decree appointing a new Muslim leader had been issued by the competent authority. Therefore, an appeal to the Supreme Court was not an effective remedy (paragraph 100).

It follows that the applicants had no effective remedy in respect of a violation of Article 9. There had thus been a violation of Article 13 of the Convention.

2.3 *Kosteski v. the Former Yugoslav Republic of Macedonia (No. 55170/00)*[8]

2.3.1 Brief Overview of the Facts of the Case

The applicant failed to report for work despite his supervisor's instructions that no employee was allowed to take days off during the week due to a heavy workload. He justified his absence by saying that he was celebrating a Muslim religious holiday which, according to the Constitution and the relevant law, was a public holiday for citizens of the Muslim faith. The authorities demanded that the applicant confirm that he was a Muslim. He could not provide such confirmation. He was subsequently subject to disciplinary sanctions, which he unsuccessfully attempted to challenge before the domestic courts. According to the applicant, his rights to freedom of conscience had been violated (Article 9 of the Convention).

2.3.2 Position of the Court

The Court did not find a violation of Article 9 of the Convention. Citing its jurisprudence, it noted that Article 9 does not protect every act motivated or inspired by religion or belief (paragraph 37). In this regard, it was not persuaded that the applicant's absence from work was a manifestation of his beliefs in the sense protected by Article 9 of the Convention, or that the imposed penalty charging him with a breach of contract by being absent without permission was an interference with those rights.

With regard to the requirement to prove one's faith, the Court recalled that an employer might consider absence without permission or apparent justification as a disciplinary offence. If the employee attempted to imply the existence of a certain privilege or right that was not usually available, then such a requirement by management was not repressive or fundamentally inconsistent with freedom of conscience. On this basis, the Court concluded that there was no violation of Article 9 in the present case.

2.3.3 Intermediate Conclusions

Through these landmark cases, the ECtHR has established a nuanced approach towards balancing religious freedoms with the obligations and requirements imposed by different professional settings.

In *Kalaç v. Turkey*, the ECtHR dealt with the dismissal of an orthodox Muslim from the Turkish military. The applicant, a judge advocate, was dismissed for his involvement in activities associated with fundamentalist religious movements.

8 Kosteski v. The former Yugoslav Republic of Macedonia—55170/00 [2006] ECHR 403 (13 April 2006).

The Court ruled that his dismissal did not violate the European Convention on Human Rights, emphasising that military service inherently involved additional requirements and obligations. These requirements were essential for maintaining discipline and cohesion within the armed forces.

The Court noted that when individuals enter military service, they must be aware of these additional constraints and the potential limitations on their religious expressions. The ECtHR upheld that the restrictions imposed by military life, including those on religious practices, were justified by the need to maintain the secular nature and operational effectiveness of the military. This case underlines the Court's recognition that certain professions, particularly those involving national security, can impose unique constraints that may limit individual freedoms, including that of religious expression.

The *Hasan and Chaush v. Bulgaria* case addressed state interference in the internal affairs of a religious community. The case involved the Bulgarian government's interference in the election and removal of a religious leader within the Muslim community, as well as its support for a faction of believers, leading to a split within the community. The ECtHR found that such interference violated Article 9 of the European Convention, which guarantees freedom of thought, conscience and religion.

The Court emphasised that the State must refrain from intervening in the internal governance of religious communities. Such interventions disrupt the autonomy of religious organisations and can lead to societal divisions. The ruling highlighted that any state actions favouring one group of believers over another could undermine social harmony and religious freedom. This case illustrates the ECtHR's commitment to protecting the internal self-governance of religious communities and preventing state actions that could exacerbate divisions within these communities.

In *Kosteski v. the Former Yugoslav Republic of Macedonia*, the applicant, a practising Muslim, was dismissed from his job for absenteeism due to religious observances. Kosteski had taken leave to celebrate a religious holiday but had not followed the proper procedures for requesting time off. The ECtHR ruled that his dismissal did not violate the European Convention, emphasising that the terms of the employment contract were binding.

The Court held that while religious beliefs must be respected, employees are also required to adhere to the terms and conditions of their employment agreements. Employers have the right to expect employees to follow established procedures, including those related to the taking of leave. This case highlights the Court's stance that religious observance does not exempt individuals from fulfilling contractual obligations. The ruling stresses the need for employees to balance their religious practices with their professional responsibilities.

These cases collectively demonstrate the ECtHR's commitment to ensuring that while religious freedoms are protected, they must be balanced with the specific requirements and obligations of various professional environments. The Ccourt's rulings highlight the importance of maintaining professional discipline and contractual obligations, preventing state interference in religious matters, and protecting the autonomy of religious communities. This nuanced approach is essential in upholding both individual rights and societal interests in diverse and pluralistic societies.

CHAPTER 7

Migration Legislation

Decisions of the European Court of Human Rights are crucial in resolving cases where migration laws conflict with the rights of Muslims. These cases frequently address complicated matters such as family separation and deportation in situations that endanger individuals' lives due to those people's religious and political convictions. The ECtHR navigates these issues with a focus on humanity and respect for human dignity, striving to balance the safeguarding of individual rights with the national interests of sovereign states.

The expulsion of migrant offenders who profess Islam often leads to the inevitable separation from their families residing in the same State. This creates significant humanitarian and legal challenges. The ECtHR has repeatedly emphasised the importance of Article 8 of the European Convention on Human Rights, which guarantees the right to respect for private and family life. However, the Court's decisions in these cases reflect a delicate balance between upholding family rights and respecting state sovereignty in immigration control.

In many instances, the ECtHR has ruled that the expulsion of a migrant offender should be weighed against the potential disruption and harm to their family life. For example, when considering the case of a migrant who has committed a serious crime, the Court must evaluate whether the individual's deportation would disproportionately impact on their family, especially if the family members are residing legally in the host country and are dependent on the migrant.

Despite the ECtHR's recognition of the significance of family unity, there is a notable tendency towards deferring to state sovereignty.[1] This deference often results in the upholding of state decisions to expel migrant offenders, even when such actions lead to family separation. The examination of these cases reveals an approach that tends to limit the protection potential of Article 8 for migrant applicants. The State's interest in maintaining public order and controlling immigration frequently outweighs the migrant's right to family life.

This judicial stance has profound implications. It stresses the Court's recognition of the legitimate aims of states to regulate immigration and ensure

---

1 Dembour, Marie-Bénédicte, 'The Migrant Case Law of the European Court of Human Rights: Critique and Way Forward', in Başak Çalı, Ledi Bianku, and Iulia Motoc, eds., *Migration and the European Convention on Human Rights* (Oxford: Oxford University Press, 2021), pp. 19–43.

national security. However, it also highlights the tension between these aims and the humanitarian considerations that the ECtHR is mandated to uphold. Consequently, while there have been landmark rulings in favour of migrants' rights, these remain exceptions rather than the rule, illustrating Strasbourg's general deference to state powers in immigration control.

The deportation of Muslim migrants who face threats to their lives for religious and political reasons in their homelands presents another complex area of jurisprudence for the ECtHR. The Court's decisions in these cases are guided by the principles of non-refoulement, which prohibit the return of individuals to a country where they are at risk of persecution or serious harm.[2]

The ECtHR has consistently upheld the principle that even individuals with a criminal background cannot be deported to countries where they would face torture, inhuman or degrading treatment, or other serious threats to their lives. This stance reflects the Court's commitment to humanism and the protection of human dignity, irrespective of the individual's criminal record or perceived threat to public security.

However, the application of this principle is not without its challenges. States often argue that granting asylum or refraining from deportation in such cases could undermine their national interests and public safety. The ECtHR must therefore carefully assess each case, balancing the individual's right to life and protection from harm with the State's sovereign right to control its borders and ensure national security.

One significant aspect of the ECtHR's approach is its rigorous scrutiny of the conditions in the migrant's country of origin. The Court examines evidence of the threat posed to the individual, considering factors such as the political and religious climate, past incidents of persecution and the credibility of the migrant's claims. This thorough assessment aims to ensure that the protection granted is justified and necessary.

Despite this rigorous approach, the Court's decisions reveal a broader trend of deference to state sovereignty in the realm of migration. While the ECtHR has issued important rulings protecting migrants' rights, these are exceptions to a general rule that often prioritises state interests in expulsion and immigration control. This trend has significant implications for migrants across the member states of the Council of Europe, highlighting the challenges of balancing human rights obligations with state sovereignty.

---

2 *Article 4 of Protocol No. 4 and Immigration Summary Returns of Migrants and/or Asylum-Seekers ('Push-backs') and Related Case Scenarios*, 2023. https://ks.echr.coe.int/documents/d/echr-ks/summary-returns-of-migrants-and-or-asylum-seekers-push-backs-and-related-case-scenarios.

This duality in the Court's approach reflects a broader tension within European migration policy. On the one hand, there is a commitment to protecting fundamental human rights, including the rights of Muslims facing persecution. On the other hand, there is a recognition of the legitimate aims of States in regulating immigration and ensuring public safety. The ECtHR's jurisprudence in this area illustrates the ongoing struggle to find a balance between these competing interests.

1 Cases Related to the Expulsion of Migrant Offenders Professing Islam and the Inevitable Separation of Their Families Living in the Same State

1.1 *Beldjoudi v. France (No. 12083/86)*[3]

1.1.1 Brief Overview of the Facts of the Case

This is one of the oldest cases in the practice of the ECtHR on cases of violation of the rights of Muslims. In this regard, it is a kind of precedent for the group of cases under consideration. The first applicant was born in France in 1950 but lost his French citizenship after Algeria gained independence in 1963. Despite this, he was brought up in France and had always lived there. Moreover, since 1970 he had been married to a French citizen, the second applicant. His entire family lived in France.

In 1969, 1974, 1977 and 1978 the first applicant was convicted of various criminal offences, including aggravated theft, for which he was sentenced to eight years' imprisonment.

In November 1979, the Minister of the Interior ordered his expulsion from the country on the grounds that his presence on French territory constituted a threat to public order. It was because of this order of the Minister of the Interior that the applicants filed a complaint with the ECtHR in which they stated that this order violated Article 8 of the Convention.

While challenging the deportation order, the first applicant committed further offences and was again brought to trial in 1986. At the same time, he unsuccessfully attempted to obtain French citizenship in 1983 and 1984.

Finally, in January 1991 the French Council of State rejected the first applicant's appeal against the Minister's order to expel him from the country. The deportation order was not carried out because the first applicant was under judicial supervision for another offence (aggravated concealment of stolen goods).

3 Beldjoudi v France—12083/86 [1992] ECHR 42 (26 March 1992).

1.1.2 Position of the Court

The Court found that there had been a violation of Article 8 of the Convention. As it noted, the impugned interference primarily concerned the applicants' joint family life as spouses (paragraph 76). Their marriage had taken place in France more than 20 years before this case began, and France had always been the place of residence of their family. The Court considered that the long time spent by the first applicant in places of detention had separated the spouses for long periods, but had nevertheless not destroyed their family life, the right to which is guaranteed in Article 8 of the Convention.

The Court also took into account the context in which the first applicant's deportation took place. Thus, having lost his citizenship as a minor, as early as in 1970, a year after his first conviction but more than nine years before the deportation order was issued, he had expressed a desire to recover his French citizenship. He was later found to be fit for national service (paragraphs 31–33, 77). In addition, he had married a French woman. All of his close relatives retained their French citizenship until 1 January 1963 and had lived in France for several decades. The Court concluded its review by stating that the first applicant had spent his entire life—more than 40 years—in France, had received a French education and did not appear to know Arabic. Thus, the Court considered that he had no connection with Algeria other than nationality.

In conclusion, the Court noted that the husband's deportation would also violate the second applicant's rights. So, to save her family, she would have to settle abroad, presumably in Algeria, a State whose language she probably did not know. Given that this would cause her considerable distress, the interference in question could jeopardize the unity or even the very existence of the marriage (paragraph 78). Therefore, the applicant's deportation would be in violation of Article 8 of the Convention.

The majority decision caused controversy among some judges. In his dissenting opinion, Judge Pettiti observed that neither the rationale of principle nor the rationale for the decision was consistent with the precise interpretation and assessment of Article 8 of the European Convention on the deportation of aliens who have committed crimes. This follows from the fact that the Convention does not limit the sovereign right of States to decide to deport from their territory aliens who have committed crimes. Likewise, the Convention does not guarantee the right of a foreigner to reside in the territory of the State in question. And the expulsion of a foreigner can be considered a violation of the Convention only in exceptional cases, but not when the applicant is a systematic offender and criminal.

Judge Pettiti opined that the fact that someone is permanently resident in the host or home country cannot be a complete bar to the exercise of the right to deport criminals. Moreover, historically close relations between the expelling country and the country of citizenship (for example, former metropolises and colonies, like France and Algeria) do not prevent deportation. From the point of view of Judge Pettiti, the right to acquire citizenship of the country of residence does not follow from such relations.

At the conclusion of his dissenting opinion, Judge Pettiti stated:

> The majority decision carries with it a source of controversy on an exponential interpretation of Article 8 if interference with the private or family life of a habitual offender is sufficient to prevent deportation, as the habitual offender position would imply. immunity in his favour. In fact, any deportation affects private or family life in the same way as any detention. If a new offence is committed, there will be further intervention. But in this case, the personal life is affected by the behavior of the person concerned.

Judge Meyer, in turn, did not argue that if the first applicant were deported there would be a violation of Article 8 of the Convention. However, in his opinion the Court did not seriously assess the legal risks of such deportation. Thus, if the first applicant, after more than 40 years, was expelled from a country that had in fact always been 'his' from the moment of birth, even if he did not possess its 'nationality', such expulsion could not be regarded as anything other than 'inhuman treatment'. Speaking about the first applicant's crimes, Judge Meyer noted that criminal punishment under French law would be fair. But not deportation.

Judge Valtikos's dissenting opinion reiterated Judge Pettiti's. The only difference was that to substantiate his position, Judge Valtikos turned to his dissenting opinion in a similar case, *Moustaquim v. Belgium* (No. 12313/86), to which the Court had also referred. Judge Valtikos noted that the applicant, being an adult who had committed serious crimes, could not be excluded from deportation on family grounds, like a teenager who had committed a series of lesser crimes. The two judges also expressed the view that the application of Article 8 of the Convention to such a case could open the door to many abuses.

Judge Martens concurred with the majority. At the same time, he went further in his reasoning and called for extending the application of paragraph 1 of Article 3 of Protocol No. 4 to the Convention, prohibiting the expulsion of citizens, to foreigners who were born and raised in a member state. Judge Martens also proposed calling such deportation an interference in personal, not family, life since 'although not all "integrated aliens" facing deportation are married, they all have a personal life.' This follows from the fact that deportation to a country where living conditions differ markedly from those in the expelling country and where the deportee, as a stranger to that land, its culture and its inhabitants, risks living in almost complete social isolation, constitutes an interference with his right to respect for his privacy.

Article 3 of Protocol 4 to the European Convention on Human Rights—Prohibition of expulsion of nationals

1. No one shall be expelled, by means either of an individual or of a collective measure, from the territory of the State of which he is a national.
2. No one shall be deprived of the right to enter the territory of the State of which he is a national.

1.2 *Yildiz and others v. Austria (No. 37295/97)*[4]

1.2.1 Brief Overview of the Facts of the Case

The applicants, a married couple and their daughter, were Turkish nationals and resided in Austria. Between 1993 and 1994 the first applicant was found guilty of several minor offences. In September 1994, the district authorities imposed a five-year ban on his residence in the country. The public security authority rejected the applicant's appeal, citing domestic law, which provided that a residence ban must be issued to a foreigner if he had been convicted more than once of similar offences by a domestic court. The Government submitted that, although the first applicant had a high degree of integration in Austria, the public interest in his being prohibited from residing in the country outweighed his interest in remaining. The applicant was unable to change this decision in court.

He was subsequently deported to Turkey in 1997. He had not committed any further offences since 1994. His residency ban expired in 1999. However, he argued that opportunities for his legal return to Austria were limited and involved long waiting periods. The applicant's wife and daughter visited him on several occasions while he was away from Austria. However, the first and second applicants divorced in 2001. The applicants complained to the European Court of Human Rights that the residence ban imposed on the first applicant had violated their right to respect for their private and family life under Article 8 of the Convention.

4 Yildiz and others v. Austria—37295/97 [2002] ECHR 701 (31 October 2002).

1.2.2 Position of the Court

The Court found a violation of Article 8 of the Convention. It held that the ban on the first applicant's residence in Austria, which resulted in his separation from his wife and child, constituted an interference with their right to respect for their private and family life (paragraph 36). However, although the applicant's expulsion was based on law and served a legitimate aim, the Court considered that the authorities had failed to strike a fair balance between the various interests involved and that the interference with the applicants' right to respect for their family life was not proportionate to the legitimate aim pursued. Accordingly, there has been a violation of Article 8 of the Convention. In particular, the minor nature of the applicant's offences, his significant integration into Austrian society and insignificant integration into Turkish society, as well as the position of his wife, who had lived in Austria all her life, were not taken into account.

1.3 *Al-Nashif v. Bulgaria (No. 50963/99)*[5]

1.3.1 Brief Overview of the Facts of the Case

The applicant, a stateless person of Palestinian origin born in Kuwait, lived in Bulgaria with his two children, who were born in Bulgaria and had Bulgarian citizenship. His permanent residence permit in Bulgaria was revoked on the ground that he was allegedly involved in religious extremism, and he was also detained and subsequently deported to Syria.

The applicant and his wife complained that his deportation constituted a violation of Articles 5(4), 8 and 13 of the Convention.

1.3.2 Position of the Court

The Court found a violation of these Articles of the Convention. It pointed out that even where national security was at stake, the concepts of legality and the rule of law in a democratic society required that measures affecting fundamental human rights be subject to some form of adversarial proceedings before an independent body competent to consider the reasons for such actions (paragraph 123).

In the present case, the respondent Government did not conduct an independent investigation into the applicant (paragraphs 21–22, 125). Moreover, the Court found that the decision to deport him was taken without him any reasons for the decision being given to him, his lawyer or any independent body competent to consider the matter (paragraph 126). Based on this, the Court con-

5 Al-Nashif v. Bulgaria—50963/99 [2002] ECHR 502 (20 June 2002).

cluded that the decision to deport was taken in accordance with a legal regime that did not provide the necessary guarantees against arbitrariness. It followed from the latter that the interference in the applicant's family life was not lawful (paragraph 128) and that there has been a violation of Article 8 of the Convention.

Judges Makarchik, Butkevich and Botucharova voted against finding a violation of Article 8 in the present case. According to them, the lack of sufficient procedural guarantees for the applicant at the domestic level did not mean that the interference with the applicants' family life was disproportionate to the legitimate aim pursued by that interference. First, it did not follow from the case that the family had sufficiently strong ties with Bulgaria (paragraph 6 of the Joint Partial Dissenting Opinion). However, the deportation was not disproportionate, given the gravity of the charges against the applicant.

For this reason, only Article 5(4) of the Convention was violated due to the improper consideration of the applicant's case by the domestic courts.

1.3.3 Intermediate Conclusions

The expulsion of migrant offenders professing Islam and the inevitable separation of their families is a highly sensitive and politicised issue in many countries. The European Court of Human Rights has addressed numerous cases that highlight the complexities of balancing individual rights with state interests in maintaining public order and security. This balance often generates significant controversy, as evidenced by the multiple dissenting opinions and comments from the judges. The ECtHR's jurisprudence in this area underlines the need to protect the family unit while acknowledging the State's right to enforce immigration laws and safeguard national security.

In *Beldjoudi v. France*, the Court addressed the case of a migrant offender who had been assimilated into French society and had a local spouse. Despite his criminal record, the Court ruled that it was impermissible to deport him due to his significant ties with France, including his marriage to a French citizen. The Court emphasised the principle of proportionality, balancing the State's interest in controlling immigration and preventing crime against the individual's right to family life under Article 8 of the European Convention on Human Rights.

The ruling highlighted the importance of considering the degree of integration and the potential impact of deportation on the individual's private and family life. This case stresses the ECtHR's stance that deportation measures must be carefully weighed against the personal circumstances and established ties of the individual to the host country.

Yildiz and Others v. Austria further illustrates the Court's approach to balancing individual and state interests. Yildiz, a migrant offender, faced deportation despite having a small child and a wife in Austria. Although Yildiz and his wife divorced during the proceedings, the Court ruled that his deportation would cause irreparable damage to his family, particularly his relationship with his child.

The ECtHR emphasised that the best interests of the child must be a primary consideration in deportation cases involving family members. It found that separating Yildiz from his child would violate his right to family life and the child's right to maintain contact with both parents. This decision reflects the Court's recognition of the profound impact that deportation can have on the family unit and the paramount importance of protecting the welfare of children in such cases.

In *Al-Nashif v. Bulgaria*, the Court addressed the case of a migrant offender involved in extremist activities with limited assimilation into the host country. Despite the serious nature of Al-Nashif's activities and his minimal integration, it ruled against his deportation due to the presence of his children who were citizens of the host country.

The Court acknowledged the State's legitimate interest in national security and combating extremism but stressed that any deportation measures must be proportional and take into account the individual's family ties and the potential impact on their children. The ECtHR found that deporting Al-Nashif would disrupt the family unit and negatively affect his children, who were citizens of the country. This case demonstrates the Court's nuanced approach, where even in situations involving serious offences, the presence of minor children with citizenship in the host country can outweigh the State's interest in deportation.

2 Deportation of Muslim Migrants When There Is a Threat to Their Lives in Their Homeland for Religious and Political Reasons

2.1 *Auad v. Bulgaria (No. 46390/10)*[6]

2.1.1 Brief Overview of the Facts of the Case

In May 2009, the applicant, a stateless person of Palestinian origin, entered Bulgaria illegally and applied for asylum, citing his fears that if he returned to Lebanon he would be killed or ill-treated by members of the Islamic militant group Jund al-Sham.

6 Auad v. Bulgaria—46390/10 [2011] ECHR 1602 (11 October 2011).

The government agency for refugees denied him refugee status but granted him humanitarian protection. However, shortly afterwards he received an expulsion order on the grounds that he was suspected of terrorism and that his presence in Bulgaria posed a serious threat to national security.

The applicant was detained pending removal to Lebanon for the maximum period of 18 months permitted by domestic law before being released. At the same time, he was limited in his ability to correspond with the outside world.

The applicant complained of a violation of Articles 3, 5 and 13 of the Convention.

2.1.2 Position of the Court

The Court found a violation of these norms. It first examined the aspect concerning the existence of a real threat to the applicant's life in Lebanon. This threat arose because of the situation in the Lebanese Palestinian refugee camp where the applicant would most likely have ended up after being deported from Bulgaria (paragraphs 102–103). Taking this into account, the Court concluded that the applicant's expulsion, if carried out, would be in violation of Article 3 of the Convention.

The Court further examined the potential for the authorities carefully to consider the question of the applicant's removal and the risks involved. In the Court's opinion, the Bulgarian Government did not indicate any procedure by which the applicant could challenge the decision to deport him, especially if it had already taken place. The legislation did not contain provisions for a specific legal action against the execution of a deportation order (paragraph 122). There had thus been a violation of Article 13 of the Convention.

Turning to the issue concerning the applicant's continued deprivation of liberty and detention, the Court held that this measure was unreasonable due to the failure of the Bulgarian court to consider whether the applicant would be at risk if returned to Lebanon. Since the detention was carried out for the purpose of the applicant's deportation, the absence of such proceedings rendered it ineffective for the entire period of the applicant's detention (paragraph 135). There had thus been a violation of Article 5(1) of the Convention.

2.2 *F.G. v. Sweden (No. 43611/11)*[7]

2.2.1 Brief Overview of the Facts of the Case

The applicant, an Iranian national, applied for asylum in Sweden in 2010 on the ground that he had worked with known opponents of the Iranian regime.

---

7 F.G. v. Sweden—43611/11—Chamber Judgment [2014] ECHR 58 (16 January 2014).

He claimed he had been arrested and detained by Iranian authorities for short periods of time at least three times between 2007 and 2009. His charges related, in particular, to his online publishing activities and participation in demonstrations. He said he had fled Iran rather than comply with a subpoena to appear in court to cooperate with the authorities against his friends.

Also, according to the applicant, after arriving in Sweden he converted to Christianity. However, he stated that his conversion was his own business, and he did not want to base his asylum claim on it.

After examining the asylum application, the Swedish authorities refused it, considering the applicant's alleged political activities to be implausible and in any case too limited to constitute a source of serious risk upon his return to Iran. In relation to his new religious beliefs, the Migration Service noted that the applicant did not wish to rely on his conversion as a basis for granting asylum and that following his faith in private was not a plausible basis for believing that he would be at risk of persecution upon return.

The applicant complained of a violation of Articles 2 and 3 of the Convention.

Article 2 of the European Convention on Human Rights—Right to life

1. Everyone's right to life shall be protected by law. No one shall be deprived of his life intentionally save in the execution of a sentence of a court following his conviction of a crime for which this penalty is provided by law.
2. Deprivation of life shall not be regarded as inflicted in contravention of this Article when it results from the use of force which is no more than absolutely necessary:
(a) in defence of any person from unlawful violence;
(b) in order to effect a lawful arrest or to prevent the escape of a person lawfully detained;
(c) in action lawfully taken for the purpose of quelling a riot or insurrection.

2.2.2 Position of the Court

The Court found a violation of Articles 2 and 3 of the Convention. It placed particular emphasis in considering the present case on the applicant's conversion to Christianity. Thus, the applicant did not wish to rely on his religious affiliation as a basis for granting asylum (paragraph 89). However, the Court concluded that there was nothing to indicate that the Iranian authorities were aware of his treatment. The Court then examined the case file and agreed with the position of the Swedish courts that there was no threat to the applicant in connection with his political activities (paragraphs 132–141).

However, all of the above, in the Court's opinion, did not exclude the authorities' obligation independently to assess the risks that the applicant might face as a result of his conversion upon return to Iran. Given the absolute nature of Articles 2 and 3 of the Convention, it was hardly possible that the person concerned could waive the protection provided under them. It followed that, regardless of the applicant's conduct, the competent national authorities were obliged, on their own initiative, to evaluate all information brought to their attention before deciding to remove him to Iran (paragraph 156).

Since the Swedish authorities had not carried out such an assessment, it would have been a violation of Articles 2 and 3 of the Convention if the applicant had been returned to Iran without an *ex nunc* assessment of the consequences of his treatment (paragraph 158).

A number of the Judges commented further on this decision. In a partly concurring and partly dissenting opinion, Judges Jöderblom and Spano opined that the applicant's reluctance to rely on his conversion to Christianity in order to claim asylum meant that he did not perceive there to be a threat from that conversion in his home country. They cited as confirmation of their words information according to which in Iran there is no persecution of Christian converts who do not demonstrate their religious affiliation.

Since there was no real risk of the applicant's persecution for his religious views (he either did not foresee the danger of his conversion and the way in which he planned to practise his new religion, or he did not intend to practise in a way that would pose a danger to him in Iran), no grounds for asylum were available for him. Judges Jöderblom and Spano noted that the applicant had been provided with a lawyer and the Migration Department had asked him about his conversion and thereby actively included this issue in the case, giving the applicant the opportunity to reflect on it.

Taking all these factors into account, the Swedish authorities cannot be accused of failing in their obligation to carry out an assessment of the relevant facts or risks during the initial asylum proceedings.

The only reason Judges Jöderblom and Spano voted for a potential violation of Articles 2 and 3 of the Convention was that the applicant had provided new material on how he would practise his religion in Iran if deported. These new circumstances indicated a risk of ill-treatment and had therefore to be taken into account by the Swedish authorities before any new decision was taken regarding his possible deportation.

Judge Jöderblom also considered that the continuation of the application was no longer justified, since the present decision of the Court had been delivered more than four years after the final decision at national level and after the expiration of the expulsion order.

In another dissenting opinion, Judge Sayo opined that the national authorities had a positive obligation to assess the situation of an asylum seeker under Articles 2 and 3 of the Convention on their own initiative, based on available information. He also proposed a separate analysis of the extent to which the Convention right freely to manifest one's religion (that is, in this case, rather than hiding one's Christian faith in Iran, as proposed by the national authorities) was extraterritorial in nature.

Judges Zimele, De Gaetano, Pinto de Albuquerque and Wojtyczek expressed a similar opinion to Judge Saio's. They added that the applicant retained his victim status even after the expiry of the deportation order and that the Swedish Migration Service continued to refuse to consider the applicant's transfer as a basis for granting him asylum, although there was information that the applicant insisted on the danger to life associated with conversion from Islam to another religion that he might face in Iran. The Judges also separately raised the issue of the inadmissibility of normalising the hidden practice of religion to avoid a threat to one's life and the existence of real threats of criminal prosecution for converting to Christianity in Iran.

2.3 *Muradi and Alieva v. Sweden* (*No. 11243/13*)[8]

2.3.1 Brief Overview of the Facts of the Case

This case is interesting because of its uncompromising and harsh nature compared to the previously discussed practice, which clearly sets it apart and makes it an important precedent. The applicants, a woman from Azerbaijan and a man from Afghanistan, approached the Swedish authorities in October 2011 with a request for asylum and a residence permit. The woman cited as reasons the risk of her becoming a victim of traffickers who persuaded her to engage in prostitution, as well as fear of her stepfather, who lived in Baku. The man, in turn, cited a threat to his life from the Taliban, who had killed his father. After studying the information provided by the applicants, their request was denied, and they were unable to challenge the decision.

A year later, the applicants again applied for asylum on the grounds that they had entered into a relationship, were expecting a child together, and could not return to Azerbaijan. The male applicant also cited his conversion to Christianity as an additional obstacle to returning to Afghanistan. The Swedish Migration Service again refused, citing the fact that no new circumstances had been

8 Muradi & Alieva v. Sweden, App. No. 11243/13 (25 June 2013).

presented that could justify the granting of a residence permit to the applicants.

Due to the risk of deportation to their home countries, in 2013 the applicants applied to the ECtHR on the basis of a violation of Articles 3, 8 and, in the case of the applicant who converted to Christianity, Article 9 of the Convention. Then their son was born. After the applicants had applied to the ECtHR, it was established that they suffered from mental disorders, were undergoing treatment in Sweden, and the second applicant, a citizen of Afghanistan, had significant bureaucratic difficulties in obtaining an Azerbaijani visa due to the lack of a passport and the inability to contact the embassy of the country of his citizenship.

2.3.2 Position of the Court

The Court declared the complaint inadmissible. It noted that the applicants' application for asylum was carefully examined by the domestic authorities and that there was no indication that those proceedings lacked effective safeguards to protect the applicants from arbitrary refoulement or were otherwise flawed (paragraph 41).

The Court further stated that there are organisations in Azerbaijan, both governmental and non-governmental, that provide centres for victims of human trafficking and shelters for women seeking protection. The first applicant was unable to demonstrate that she would not receive protection from the authorities of Azerbaijan, a member state of the Council of Europe, in respect of any threats from private individuals (paragraph 42). As regards the second applicant, the Court also found his arguments about the threat to him from the Taliban to be unfounded (paragraph 43). Thus, no violation of Article 3 of the Convention has been established.

The Court was also not convinced by the applicant's arguments about his conversion to Christianity (this happened after the Migration Board rejected his application for asylum). Moreover, it found it significant that he did not mention conversion in his appeals, although he must have been aware of its importance (paragraph 44). In this respect, the Court took a position opposite to that it took in the previous case, *FG v. Sweden*. In addition, it concluded that the first applicant was not at risk of ill-treatment in Azerbaijan (paragraph 46), but the mental health of both applicants was primarily related to the asylum process rather than to the perceived risks in Azerbaijan and Afghanistan (paragraph 47).

In conclusion, the Court considered that there had been no violation of Article 8 of the Convention since the Swedish authorities had pursued a legitimate aim and the applicants had had the opportunity to move to one country. The

Court considered the bureaucratic difficulties of one of the applicants to be an unduly serious obstacle if the applicants had the goal of preserving their family. In any case, this was not the responsibility of the Swedish authorities (paragraph 52).

The Court based the absence of a violation of Article 9 of the Convention on the fact that it had not been proven that the second applicant would not be able to raise his son in the Christian tradition if he were deported from Sweden. In the light of the above, this part of the application was declared inadmissible pursuant to Article 35(3)(a) and 4 of the Convention.

2.3.3 Intermediate Conclusions

The deportation of Muslim migrants facing threats to their lives in their homeland for religious and political reasons presents a complex and contentious issue. The European Court of Human Rights has developed a nuanced approach to such cases, balancing state sovereignty and immigration control with the protection of fundamental human rights. This selection of cases highlights the flexibility of the ECtHR's approach, which has led to significant disagreements among the judges due to the high politicisation of the issue.

In *Auad v. Bulgaria*, the Court examined the case of an illegal migrant facing deportation to a country where his life would be at risk. The ECtHR ruled that deportation in such circumstances would violate Article 3 of the European Convention on Human Rights, which prohibits inhuman or degrading treatment. The Court emphasised that States have an obligation to conduct their own investigations to assess the risk to the individual's life upon return. The ECtHR's decision in *Auad v. Bulgaria* emphasised the importance of a thorough and individualised risk assessment by the deporting State. This includes evaluating the political and security situation in the country of origin and considering any evidence provided by the migrant.

In *FG v. Sweden*, the Court dealt with the deportation of a migrant who had converted from Islam to Christianity. The ECtHR ruled that, before deporting such an individual, the State must ensure that the change of religion would not lead to negative consequences in the country of origin. This obligation persists even if the migrant does not explicitly cite the change of religion as a reason for asylum. The Court's decision in *FG v. Sweden* highlights the need for States proactively to investigate potential risks associated with a migrant's conversion to another religion.

In this case the ECtHR also addressed cases where migrants face deportation despite claims of political activism that might endanger their lives. In such cases, the Court considers whether the migrant's identity and activities have been kept confidential. If the individual's political activities are considered insignificant and unlikely to be known in the country of origin, deportation may be considered permissible.

In *Muradi and Alieva v. Sweden*, the Court explored the possibility of deporting migrants to a third country where they might not face direct persecution but could encounter other significant difficulties. The ECtHR allowed for the possibility of refusing asylum to and deporting individuals if they had the opportunity to remain in a third country, despite poor integration, family difficulties, health problems and bureaucratic obstacles.

This ruling marks a significant departure from the Court's typical emphasis on the immediate risks posed by deportation. It acknowledges that, in some cases, the availability of a third country as an alternative destination might justify deportation, even if the conditions in that third country are not ideal. This decision underscores the ECtHR's pragmatic approach to complex migration issues, though it has sparked debate about the adequacy of protections in third countries.

In conclusion, the ECtHR's approach to the deportation of Muslim migrants stresses the importance of individualised assessments and the need for States to fulfil their obligations under international human rights law. While the Court's rulings have provided critical protections for vulnerable individuals, they have also highlighted the challenges and contentious nature of balancing these protections with broader political and practical considerations.

CHAPTER 8

Restriction of Muslims in the Ability to Perform Religious Duties

In examining how the right to perform Islamic rituals is dealt with in the jurisprudence of the European Court of Human Rights concerning violations of the religious freedoms of Muslims, we must consider the practice of religion both outside sacred places and within religious and sacred locations. This division is essential as the territorial factor plays a significant role in determining legal consequences.

Muslim daily practices are religious in nature, and adherents consider many of these practices obligatory, forming an integral part of their religious identity.[1] Consequently, in a number of countries, religious freedom for Muslims goes beyond the mere ability to practise their religion freely; it also encompasses compliance with Sharia law in matters such as marriage and family relations.

The right to the undisturbed practice of religious worship entails that individuals should not face obstacles or restrictions in performing their religious duties. Moreover, this right imposes upon the state the obligation not only to refrain from violating religious freedoms itself but also to prevent violations by third parties.[2] Thus, the State is tasked with safeguarding the freedom of religious worship for all individuals, including Muslims.

In cases brought before the European Court of Human Rights regarding violations of the religious freedoms of Muslims, the Court has consistently upheld the principle that individuals should be able to practise their religion freely and without interference. This includes the right to perform Islamic rituals both within and outside sacred places. The Court recognises the importance of ensuring that Muslims can engage in religious practices such as prayer, fasting and other observances, regardless of location, without hindrance or restriction. The ECtHR's jurisprudence emphasises that religious rights are not limited to

1 Zuriet, Jade, and Lyausheva, Svetlana, 'Muslim Identity in the Conceptual Field of Modern Religious Studies,' *SHS Web of Conferences*, vol. 72, 2019, p. 02008. https://doi.org/10.1051/shsconf/20197202008.

2 Martínez-Torrón, Javier, 'Islam in Strasbourg: Can Politics Substitute for Law?' in W. Cole Durham, ed., *Islam, Europe and Emerging Legal Issues* (Farnham: Ashgate, 2012), pp. 19–24.

sacred spaces like mosques but extend to other settings, including places of detention.

Within sacred places such as mosques, the ECtHR stresses the need for Muslims to exercise their religious rights, attend religious services, participate in rituals and engage in communal worship without obstruction. This extends to the broader principle of religious freedom that the Court has consistently defended, highlighting the necessity of balancing these rights with security and administrative concerns, particularly in the context of detention facilities.

The ECtHR's jurisprudence demonstrates that any restrictions on religious practices must be justifiable, necessary and proportionate. The Court has emphasised that the State has a duty to protect individuals from interference with their religious practices, particularly by third parties. This includes safeguarding against discrimination, harassment or violence based on religious beliefs. The Court's decisions have been clear in establishing that any restrictions placed on religious practices—whether inside or outside detention—must respect the fundamental rights of prisoners and the broader principle of religious freedom.

A key area of concern in the context of Muslim religious practices is the issue of halal food and religious slaughter. Islamic slaughter, or halal animal slaughter, is a relatively rare issue in the jurisprudence of the ECtHR. While cases involving religious slaughter typically involve Jewish practices, the Court has considered a case specifically related to Islamic slaughter. This case stands out as the only instance involving the Islamic faith in the ECtHR's practice and warrants separate attention, particularly in discussions on the restrictions faced by Muslims in the exercise of their religious duties.

This case represents an extension of the ongoing issue of dietary restrictions faced by Muslim prisoners, as seen in other cases concerning access to halal food during incarceration. The ECtHR has considered how state authorities balance the protection of religious freedoms with other considerations, such as security and public policy. The rarity of Islamic slaughter cases reflects the broader challenge of ensuring that detainees' rights are respected while maintaining the operational requirements of detention facilities. The Court's decisions emphasise that while public order must be protected, any limitations on religious practices must be justified and proportionate, ensuring that individuals' ability to practise their faith is not disproportionately affected.

The ECtHR places particular importance on the status of the victim in such cases, requiring applicants to demonstrate that they have suffered as a direct result of the violation. This approach ensures that the Court's judgments are grounded in the protection of individual freedoms and liberties. By ensuring that only those who experience tangible harm can claim a violation, the Court reinforces its commitment to safeguarding the rights and dignity of individuals within its jurisdiction, including those practising Islam. Through this body of jurisprudence, the ECtHR has emphasised the necessity of respecting and protecting religious rights, even within the confines of detention, and promoting tolerance and pluralism in European societies.

In reviewing the existing case law, we have categorised the violations of Muslims' religious freedoms into three primary groups: Violation of Muslims' Rights to Perform Religious Duties in Places of Detention, Violation of the Right to Perform Islamic Rituals in Mosques and Other Holy Places of Islam and Islamic Slaughter. The first two groups reflect the common themes within the ECtHR's jurisprudence on the issue. Additionally, we have separately highlighted the case concerning Islamic Slaughter, specifically halal animal slaughter, as it addresses a rare but significant issue related to Muslims' religious practices. This division aims to provide a clearer understanding of how the Court has dealt with religious freedoms in different contexts, ensuring a balance between religious rights and other public interests.

1 Violation of Muslims' Rights to Perform Religious Duties in Places of Detention

1.1 *Korostelev v. Russia* (*No. 29290/10*)[3]

1.1.1 Brief Overview of the Facts of the Case

This and the next case involve instances where Muslims serving prison sentences were not allowed to perform night prayers prescribed by the rules of Islam due to internal regulations. In the present case, the applicant, who was serving a life sentence and had converted to Islam in prison, complained that the regulation of the prison does not allow him to perform night prayers and constitutes a breach of Article 9 of the ECtHR.

1.1.2 Position of the Court

The Court found a violation of Article 9 of the Convention. It reiterated that while in detention prisoners continue to enjoy all fundamental rights and freedoms, with the exception of the right to liberty (paragraph 52). It found that the only reason for the applicant's disciplinary action was the formal incompatibility of his actions with the prison regulations (paragraph 58). According to the Court, such a formalist approach clearly ignored the applicant's individual

3 Korostelev v. Russia—29290/10 [2020] ECHR 314 (12 May 2020).

situation and did not take into account the requirement to strike a fair balance between competing private and public interests.

Given the absence of any negative consequences or disturbance surrounding the applicant's religious observances, there has been a violation of Article 9 of the Convention.

1.2 *Abdullah Yalcin (No. 2) v. Türkiye (No. 34417/10)*[4]

1.2.1 Brief Overview of the Facts of the Case

This case is in many ways similar to the previous one, the only difference being that here the applicant applied to the management of a high-security prison for permission to conduct collective Friday prayers for prisoners and to allocate a separate room for these needs. The applicant considered the refusal to be a violation of Article 9 of the Convention.

1.2.2 Position of the Court

The Court again found that there had been a violation of Article 9 of the Convention. In its opinion, the strict regime of the applicant's prison did not in itself exclude the possibility of satisfying the applicant's request to the prison management (paragraph 32). It also found that the authorities had not assessed whether the gathering of a certain number of prisoners for Friday prayers might, in the individual circumstances of the case, create a security risk (paragraph 33).

On the basis that the respondent Government had failed to demonstrate that the national authorities had weighed any competing interests by giving relevant and sufficient reasons in a manner consistent with their positive obligations, there was a violation of Article 9 of the Convention.

1.3 *Neagu v. Romania (No. 21969/15)*[5]

1.3.1 Brief Overview of the Facts of the Case

The applicant, during his imprisonment, converted to Islam and asked the prison authorities to adjust his diet in accordance with the dietary requirements of Islam. The prison authorities demanded that the applicant provide confirmation of his conversion to Islam and subsequently denied his request. On this basis, the applicant filed a complaint alleging a violation of Article 9 of the Convention.

---

4 Abdullah Yalcin (No. 2) v. Türkiye—34417/10 [2022] ECHR 473 (14 June 2022).

5 Neagu v. Romania—21969/15 French Text [2020] ECHR 799 (10 November 2020).

1.3.2 Position of the Court

The Court found a violation of Article 9 of the Convention. In its opinion, a regulation with a strict requirement for documentary evidence of affiliation with a particular religion exceeds the level of justification that may be required for genuine religious belief. This is also confirmed by the fact that the prisoner had the initial freedom to practise a religion without any evidence being necessary (paragraph 9). The Court found that the domestic courts had not examined whether the applicant had a real possibility of obtaining written or other evidence of membership of the relevant religion, particularly in view of the restrictions to which he was subjected as a prisoner (paragraph 40).

The Court rejected the respondent Government's argument that the applicant had changed his religion for a second time, as evidenced by the fact that he had requested meals consistent with dietary standards specific to the Adventist faith (paragraph 19), on the basis that the domestic courts had not considered that this request was an abuse on his part (paragraph 42).

The Court stated that the domestic authorities had failed to strike the fair balance which they should have struck, balancing the interests of the prison establishment, of other prisoners and the special interests of the prisoner concerned, and that there had therefore been a violation of Article 9 of the Convention.

Disagreeing with this decision, Judges Pakzolay and Grozev issued a dissenting opinion. According to them, in this case the requirement to provide a document of conversion to Islam was not excessive, since Romanian legislation provides for the initial registration of a prisoner's religious affiliation upon his arrival in prison, and that this does not require documentary confirmation. A more complex procedure for taking religion into account when changing religion, requiring an act of confirmation by a representative of the relevant religion or religious association, was aimed at preventing abuse.

Considering that at the beginning of his detention the applicant indicated that he belonged to the Orthodox Christian Church, and then, twice in three years, he changed his faith, the sincerity of his transition was doubtful. Moreover, the applicant had had the opportunity to provide the necessary document declaring his conversion to Islam in the presence of the imam and witnesses. However, this was not done.

All these circumstances together, according to Judges Pakzolay and Grozev, indicate that there was no violation of Article 9 of the Convention.

1.4 *Saran v. Romania (No. 65993/16)*[6]

1.4.1 Brief Overview of the Facts of the Case

This case is similar to *Neagu v. Romania*, where the applicant was required to provide evidence of his religious conversion during detention in order to receive meals compatible with his Muslim faith. This requirement interfered with his right freely to practise his religion, as protected under Article 9 of the ECtHR.

1.4.2 Position of the Court

In its decision, the Court noted that the applicant had confirmed he was provided with food in accordance with Muslim religious prescriptions at the beginning of his detention and was registered as a Muslim in the relevant documents (paragraph 39). However, despite this, the first instance court rejected his appeal, stating that the applicant had declared himself a Christian at the start of his detention and failed to provide evidence of his Muslim faith (paragraph 40). The Court also emphasised that the national authorities had not explained the discrepancies in the applicant's religious affiliation documents and had not attempted to verify the facts recorded by the administration (paragraph 40).

The Court concluded that the refusal to provide food in accordance with the applicant's religious prescriptions violated his right to freedom of religion, as the national authorities failed to balance the interests of the institution, those of other detainees and the applicant's specific needs (paragraph 41). Additionally, the delay in processing the food request was deemed unacceptable, given that the decision was made in March 2017, despite the applicant's transfer to another prison in December 2016 (paragraph 42). As a result, the Court found that the national authorities did not fulfil their positive obligations to provide food that took account of the applicant's religious beliefs and ruled that there was a violation of Article 9 of the Convention (paragraphs 43–44).

1.4.3 Intermediate Conclusions

In conclusion, the European Court of Human Rights has consistently reinforced the right of Muslim individuals to perform religious rituals, including in places of detention, thereby upholding the principle of religious freedom in a variety of settings. The Court's approach reflects a nuanced understanding that while security and administrative considerations within detention facilities are legitimate, they should not result in an undue restriction of fundamental rights,

6 Saran v. Romania, No. 65993/16, ECtHR (Fourth Section) (10 November 2020).

particularly religious freedoms. The ECtHR has made it clear that the right to manifest one's religion, as guaranteed by Article 9 of the European Convention on Human Rights, extends to practices such as performing Salah (Islamic prayers) or observing other religious duties, even when such practices conflict with the internal rules of detention centres.

The case of *Korostelev v. Russia* is a prime example of the Court's stance on this issue. In this case, a Muslim prisoner was penalised for performing Salah during hours when it was not allowed according to the prison's internal rules. The Court ruled that these disciplinary actions violated the prisoner's right to freedom of thought, conscience and religion, emphasising that religious rituals are an integral aspect of religious freedom. While acknowledging that prisons must account for security needs and operational concerns, the Court emphasised that these concerns should not trump the fundamental right of individuals to practise their religion, and reasonable accommodations must be made to allow prisoners to observe their faith. This case illustrates the ECtHR's commitment to ensuring that religious practices, even within the confines of detention, are protected.

Similarly, in *Abdullah Yalçin (No. 2) v. Turkey*, the Court addressed a situation where a Muslim prisoner asked to perform specific Islamic rituals that conflicted with the prison's security protocols. The Court acknowledged that security concerns are legitimate, but it also emphasised that prison authorities are required to consider carefully the religious needs of prisoners and make accommodations where feasible. In this case, the Court reiterated that restrictions on religious practices must meet the standards of necessity and proportionality. The authorities were required to assess each request individually, providing justifiable reasons for any limitations imposed, and ensuring that the religious rights of prisoners were not unnecessarily compromised. This ruling further stresses the need for a balanced approach that respects both the rights of prisoners to practice their religion and the security requirements of detention facilities.

Furthermore, *Neagu v. Romania* and *Saran v. Romania* demonstrate similar issues regarding the right to practise religion while in detention, particularly related to the requirement of providing documentary evidence for religious conversion. In *Neagu v. Romania*, the applicant's request for meals compatible with his Muslim faith was denied because he was required to prove his conversion to Islam through documentation. The Court found this to be a violation of Article 9, stating that the requirement of documentary evidence of religious affiliation was an unjustified restriction on the freedom to manifest one's religion. Similarly, in *Saran v. Romania*, the applicant faced similar challenges in asserting his Muslim identity to receive meals according to his faith. The Court ruled that the national authorities had failed to balance the prison's interests and the applicant's religious needs, ultimately finding a violation of Article 9.

Through these and other cases, the ECtHR has established a clear and consistent approach to the issue of religious freedoms in detention. The Court recognises that while detention facilities must balance security and administrative concerns, this should not come at the expense of prisoners' religious rights. Any restrictions placed on religious practices must be justifiable, necessary and proportionate, ensuring that prisoners' fundamental rights are respected. The Court's decisions highlight the obligation of state authorities to make reasonable accommodations for the religious needs of Muslim prisoners, ensuring that restrictions on religious practices are not arbitrary or overly restrictive. This body of jurisprudence demonstrates the ECtHR's commitment to upholding religious freedom, even in the context of detention, and reflects the broader principle that religious rights should be protected in all settings, including places of confinement.

2 Violation of the Right to Perform Islamic Rituals in Mosques and Other Holy Places of Islam

2.1 *Ouardiri v. Switzerland* (*No. 65840/09*)[7]

2.1.1 Brief Overview of the Facts of the Case

The following two cases concern unsuccessful attempts by Islamic communities and activists to challenge the legal ban on the construction of minarets.

In November 2009, Switzerland amended its constitution to prohibit the construction of minarets. This amendment was adopted in a popular referendum, in which supporters of the ban justified their position by the fact that the minaret is a symbol of Islamic expansionism. The applicant, a minister of one of the mosques who lived in Switzerland, alleged a violation of Articles 9 and 14 of the Convention.

2.1.2 Position of the Court

The Court rejected the complaint on the ground that the applicant was not a victim of the minaret ban established by the referendum. It pointed out that, according to Article 34 of the Convention, the concept of victim referred to direct victims of the alleged violation, that is, the people directly affected by the facts allegedly constituting the interference, and not to those who merely

7 Ouardiri v. Switzerland—65840/09 (28 June 2011).

had an interest. In any case, whether the victim was direct, indirect or potential, there had to be a connection between the complainant and the harm he believed he had suffered as a result of the alleged violation.

In the present case, the Court noted that the applicant essentially complained that the challenged constitutional provision offended his religious beliefs, without indicating any impact the prohibition had on him. Therefore, the Court concluded that the applicant was not a victim. Accordingly, his complaint alleging a violation of Articles 9 and 14 of the Convention had to be rejected in accordance with Article 35(3) and 4 of the Convention.

2.2 *Association Ligue des Muslims de Suisse and Others v. Switzerland (No. 66274/09)*[8]

2.2.1 Brief Overview of the Facts of the Case

A similar complaint was filed by the applicant, an association of Swiss Muslims.

2.2.2 Position of the Court

The Court rejected this complaint on the same grounds. It stated that associations cannot claim themselves to be victims of measures that would violate the rights that the Convention recognises for its members. The Court noted that the applicant association did not seek to build mosques equipped with minarets, nor did it state that it intended to construct such buildings in the future. It was therefore not a direct victim of the alleged violation of the Convention. As in the previous case, the application was rejected in accordance with Article 35(3) and (4) of the Convention.

2.3 *Karaahmed v. Bulgaria (No. 30587/13)*[9]

2.3.1 Brief Overview of the Facts of the Case

This case is vaguely reminiscent of the Georgian case, *Muslim Relations and Others v. Georgia*, the only difference being that here Islamophobic attacks by protesters took place near a mosque during Friday prayers. In the present case, followers of a political party with anti-Islamic rhetoric staged a rally near a mosque, shouting offensive slogans and committing many other actions directed against believers (for example, setting prayer rugs on fire and throwing eggs at worshippers).

The applicant, who took part in the disruption of Friday prayers, appealed to the ECtHR with a complaint about a violation of Article 3 (humiliation of

8 Ligue des Muslims de Suisse and Others v. Switzerland—66274/09 and 06/28/2011 [date?].

9 Karaahmed v. Bulgaria—30587/13—[2015] ECHR 217 (24 February 2015).

human dignity) separately or in combination with Articles 14, and 9 of the Convention.

2.3.2 Position of the Court

The Court found a violation of only Article 9 of the Convention. Regarding the violation of Article 3, the Court stated that, although the demonstrators' intentions went beyond mere protest and were aimed at publicly ridiculing and humiliating believers, they were not so serious as to cause the kind of fear, anguish or inferiority that were necessary for the application of this Article of the Convention (paragraph 75). The Court therefore concluded that the threshold of Article 3 had not been met in this case. As stated above, this finding made it unnecessary to consider whether the Government had complied with its positive obligations under this provision. It followed that this complaint was manifestly ill-founded and had to be rejected in accordance with Article 35(3)(a) and (4) of the Convention.

As regards the violation of Article 9, the Court held that the authorities had failed to take any action to prevent clashes between believers and demonstrators, although such an outcome was obvious, given their party's well-known policy towards Islam (paragraphs 100–102). It was the demonstrators' proximity to the mosque—with so few police between them and the worshippers—that allowed the demonstrators to cause unrest. However, the government subsequently also failed to provide a thorough investigation into the incident and did not seek to bring the protesters to justice (paragraph 110).

This failure of the national authorities to strike an appropriate balance of public interests and their subsequent failure to respond appropriately to these events meant that the State had failed to fulfil its positive obligations under Article 9.

2.3.3 Intermediate Conclusions

The European Court of Human Rights has addressed various cases involving the right to practise Islamic worship at mosques and other sacred places, balancing the protection of religious freedoms with other societal interests.

In *Ouardiri v. Switzerland* and *Association Ligue des Muslims de Suisse and Others v. Switzerland*, the ECtHR considered the implications of a Swiss constitutional amendment banning the construction of minarets. The applicants argued that the ban violated their rights under the European Convention on Human Rights. However, the Court dismissed their complaints on procedural grounds, stating that the applicants were not 'victims' within the meaning of the Convention because they had not demonstrated an intention to construct minarets.

The Court noted that the ban did not directly affect the applicants' ability to practise their religion, as it did not prevent them from constructing mosques or other places of worship without minarets. Consequently, it held that there was no interference with their right to freedom of religion under Article 9 of the Convention.

In *Karaahmed v. Bulgaria*, the ECtHR addressed the issue of anti-Islamic demonstrations near a mosque in Sofia. It found that the Bulgarian authorities had failed adequately to protect the worshippers' right to practise their religion free from harassment and intimidation. It was held that the State had a positive obligation to ensure that individuals could practise their religion in conditions that respected their freedom of thought, conscience and religion. By failing to prevent the disruptive demonstrations, the authorities had violated Article 9 of the Convention. However, the Court noted that the anti-Islamic demonstration near the mosque on Fridays did not constitute cruel treatment of believers but still violated their religious freedom. This distinction emphasises the Court's nuanced approach to balancing freedom of expression with the right to religious practice.

The Court's decisions demonstrate its careful consideration of the context and impact of restrictions on religious practices. While it recognises the importance of protecting public order, it also stresses the need for States to justify any limitations on religious freedom and to ensure that such measures do not disproportionately affect the ability of individuals to practise their faith.

In these cases, the European Court of Human Rights places particular emphasis on the status of the victim. To be granted the status of a victim, applicants must demonstrate that they have suffered as a direct result of the alleged violation. This entails showing a personal interest that has been adversely affected by the violation complained of. Importantly, the status of a victim is reserved for individuals who have experienced tangible harm or detriment due to the violation, and complaints based solely on the protection of public interests are deemed inadmissible.

The ECtHR's emphasis on the status of the victim underlines its commitment to upholding personal rights and religious rituals. By requiring applicants to demonstrate a direct and personal interest in the case, the Court ensures that its judgments are grounded in the protection of individual freedoms and liberties. This approach reflects the ECtHR's broader mandate to safeguard the rights and dignity of all individuals within its jurisdiction, including those practising Islam and engaging in religious rituals.

3 Islamic Slaughter

Islamic slaughter, or the practice of halal animal slaughter, is a relatively rare issue in the jurisprudence of the European Court of Human Rights. While cases involving religious slaughter typically involve Jewish practices, the ECtHR has considered a case related to Islamic slaughter, which stands out as the only case in the Court's practice concerning the Islamic faith.[10] This case warrants separate attention in the context of the broader discussion on restrictions faced by Muslims in the exercise of their religious duties, particularly when it intersects with issues such as religious dietary practices and the challenges of adhering to religious obligations while in detention.

The case thus represents an extension to the ongoing issue of dietary restrictions faced by Muslim prisoners, as seen in other cases concerning access to halal food during incarceration. It highlights how state authorities must navigate the balance between religious freedoms and other considerations, including between security and public policy, when regulating the religious practices of detainees. While the Court has acknowledged the importance of accommodating religious needs, the rarity of Islamic slaughter cases reflects the broader challenge of ensuring that detainees' rights are respected without unduly imposing burdens on prison systems or violating national regulations.

3.1 *Executief van de Moslims van België and Others v. Belgium (No. 16760/22, 16849/22, 16850/22)*[11]

3.1.1 Brief Overview of the Facts of the Case

The applicants were 13 Belgian nationals and seven NGOs representing Belgium's Muslim and Jewish communities, including national and local religious authorities. In Belgium, the former section 16 of the Law of 14 August 1986 on animal protection prohibits the slaughtering of vertebrates without stunning, except for religious rites. However, following a 2014 reform, animal welfare became a regional competence. As a result, the Flemish and Walloon Regions ended the exception for ritual slaughter without stunning, while the Brussels Capital Region retained it.

Several applicants challenged the decrees in the Constitutional Court, which referred questions to the Court of Justice of the European Union (CJEU). In

---

10 *Guide on Article 9 of the European Convention on Human Rights—Freedom of Thought, Conscience and Religion*, updated on 31 August 2024. Council of Europe/European Court of Human Rights, 2024, pp. 36–37.

11 Executief van de Moslims van België and Others v. Belgium—16760/22, 16849/22, 16850/22 et al. [Section II] (13 February 2024).

2020, the CJEU ruled that EU law did not prevent member states from requiring reversible stunning in ritual slaughter. Reversible stunning is a technique in which the animal is temporarily rendered unconscious without being killed, allowing it to recover before the slaughter process begins. This method is considered acceptable in halal slaughter by some Muslims, as it ensures the animal is alive when its blood begins to drain, which is a key requirement in the Islamic slaughtering process. The Constitutional Court later dismissed the applicants' case. The applicants complained that the ban violated their right to freedom of religion under Article 9, arguing that it made it difficult or impossible for Jewish and Muslim believers to practise their faith. They also claimed discrimination under Article 14 in conjunction with Article 9.

3.1.2 Position of the Court

The applicants raised two main grievances: firstly, the prohibition under the disputed decrees on slaughtering animals in accordance with religious precepts and, secondly, the difficulty or even impossibility of obtaining meat from animals slaughtered according to these religious practices (paragraph 64).

In this decision, the European Court of Human Rights examined whether the ban on ritual slaughter without prior stunning, introduced in two regions of Belgium, violated the freedom of religion of Muslims and Jews. The Court reiterated that the Convention mechanism was fundamentally subsidiary, meaning that national authorities had democratic legitimacy and were generally better placed to understand local needs and contexts (paragraph 104). It also emphasised that matters of public policy, especially those concerning the relationship between the State and religions, required special deference to decisions made by national authorities (paragraph 105). However, such restrictions on freedom of religion had to be justified and proportional to legitimate aims, such as protecting public morals (paragraph 106).

The Court noted that although the Convention does not explicitly protect animal welfare as a fundamental right, it can be linked to the protection of public morals, which provides the basis for national authorities to intervene in religious practices when necessary to reduce animal suffering (paragraph 107). Specifically, it pointed out that the ban on slaughter without stunning was enacted after thorough consultations with various stakeholders, including religious groups and animal welfare organisations, with legislative bodies carefully weighing the rights and interests of all parties involved (paragraph 109).

Regarding the national judicial review, the Court observed that the national courts had issued well-reasoned decisions based on the European Court's case law. Importantly, before making its ruling the Belgian Constitutional Court had referred the case to the Court of Justice of the European Union (CJEU), which confirmed the compatibility of the measure with EU law (paragraphs 112–114). The Court stressed that, given this dual level of scrutiny, it had to respect the principle of subsidiarity, which underpins the Convention (paragraph 115).

Concerning whether the stunning procedure was necessary for animal welfare, the Court noted that scientific evidence and consultations with experts indicated that stunning prior to slaughter was the most effective way to reduce animal suffering (paragraph 116). It observed that the Belgian lawmakers, when enacting the measures, had sought to find a compromise that took into account both religious rights and the need to protect animals (paragraphs 118–119).

As for the second part of the applicants' complaint, which concerned the difficulty or even impossibility of obtaining meat in accordance with their religious beliefs, the Court noted that the ban did not extend to meat sourced from other countries or regions where stunning was not a legal requirement. Moreover, the applicants had not demonstrated that access to meat slaughtered in accordance with their religious beliefs had become more difficult after the enactment of the decrees (paragraph 122).

In conclusion, the Court found that by adopting measures that regulated ritual slaughter with mandatory stunning, the Belgian authorities had not exceeded the margin of appreciation available to them under Article 9 of the Convention. The measures were justified in principle and proportional to the aim of protecting animal welfare as part of public morals, while also considering the rights of religious groups (paragraph 123).

In her concurring opinion, Judge Koskelo, supported by Judge Kūris, agreed with the judgment in the case but highlighted one aspect of the reasoning that, while not decisive in this specific case, was of a more general nature. The issue concerned paragraph 117 of the judgment, which suggests that a measure can meet the proportionality criterion under the Convention (specifically under Article 9 § 2) only if the legitimate goal could not be achieved through less restrictive or intrusive measures. Judge Koskelo found this problematic, as it contradicted the Court's established jurisprudence, particularly in several recent Grand Chamber judgments, and did not align with key principles like the margin of appreciation and subsidiarity. She referred to previous rulings, such as *Animal Defenders International v. UK* (2013) and *Vavřička v. Czech Republic* (2021), which emphasised that the core issue was not whether less restrictive measures could have been adopted but whether the national authorities had acted within their margin of appreciation when balancing competing interests. She argued that applying a stricter proportionality test—requiring proof that no less restrictive measure could have achieved the legitimate aim—would undermine the concept of margin of appreciation, especially in cases involving legislative measures. While acknowledging the Court's recognition of the State's wide margin of appreciation in this case, she disagreed with any suggestion that the proportionality analysis should consider the availability of less restrictive measures, as it would be inconsistent with the Court's general approach to proportionality.

In her turn, Judge Yüksel agrees with the conclusion that there had been no violation of Article 9, but she raised concerns regarding the reasoning behind the judgment. The case concerned Belgian regulations requiring pre-slaughter stunning which, the applicants argued, interfered with their right to conduct ritual slaughter in accordance with their religious practices. The key issues were whether animal welfare could be considered a legitimate aim under Article 9 and whether the measure was proportionate.

While she acknowledges that animal welfare could be a legitimate aim, Judge Yüksel criticised the Court's focus on whether the measure was the least restrictive. She argued that the Court should focus instead on whether the authorities had properly balanced the competing interests, rather than questioning what aspects of ritual slaughter were essential, a question that ought to be left to religious practitioners and theologians. She emphasised that the proportionality assessment should centre on whether the authorities achieved a proper balance between religious freedom and public morals, in accordance with established case law.

CHAPTER 9

Burial and Cemeteries: Violation of Muslims' Religious Rights in the Area of Handling the Bodies of the Dead

The question of how to treat the dead has long been a contentious issue across various cultures and legal systems. Despite widespread recognition that the dead deserve respectful treatment, numerous conflicts arise regarding burial practices, autopsies and the handling of deceased bodies, particularly in multicultural societies. This complexity becomes evident particularly when religious beliefs clash with public policy or legal requirements. In the context of Islam, the handling of the dead is governed by specific religious laws and practices that aim to honour the deceased, with burial being one of the key rites. For Muslims, the proper disposal of the body is not only a matter of respect but also a religious obligation with profound spiritual significance.[1]

The European Court of Human Rights has addressed several cases related to the violation of religious freedoms in the context of handling the bodies of the dead, particularly in situations involving Muslim practices. While legal systems, especially within the common law tradition, have historically regarded the dead as lacking 'personhood' and considered the disposal of the body as a matter of property and family rights,[2] Islamic law sees the treatment of the dead as a matter of profound religious duty, with specific rules that must be adhered to for a proper burial.[3] The importance of these practices cannot be overstated, as they are viewed as a continuation of religious observance, even after death.

One of the key issues arising in cases involving Muslims' rights to handle the bodies of the deceased is the performance of autopsies, particularly when families object for religious reasons. In Islamic law, autopsies are generally prohibited unless required for legal or security reasons, such as suspicion of foul play or public health threats. The ECtHR has been tasked with balancing the

1 See, e.g., Moazam, Farhat, *Bioethics and Organ Transplantation in a Muslim Society: A Study in Culture, Ethnography, and Religion* (Bloomington: Indiana University Press, 2006).

2 Shevelev, Arseny, and Shevelev, Georgy, 'The Nature of the Right in a Dead Body Revisited: A Study in Comparative Legal Ideas,'*Louisiana Law Review* 83.4 (2023), p. 9.

3 Halevi, Leor, *Muhammad's Grave: Death Rites and the Making of Islamic Society* (New York: Columbia University Press, 2011), p. 75.

State's interest in forensic investigations, including autopsies, with the religious rights of Muslim families who object to such practices on the ground of their faith. This tension between public health and religious obligations has led to several legal disputes. These disputes highlight the need for the Court to consider carefully the cultural and religious significance of burial practices and the handling of bodies in cases where Muslims are involved.[4]

In certain circumstances, as seen in the case of Islamic slaughter, the Court has recognised that States must accommodate religious practices, even when they may conflict with the interests of public health or security. In the context of burial and the treatment of the dead, the same principle applies. The ECtHR has stressed that restrictions on religious practices, including those related to death rituals, must be justifiable, necessary and proportionate. This means that when public authorities impose restrictions on burial practices, they must ensure that the religious rights of individuals are not unnecessarily compromised.

Notably, there have been cases in which Muslim communities have challenged the practice of autopsies or the handling of deceased bodies in ways that conflicted with Islamic funeral rites. These legal battles often arise when authorities do not make reasonable accommodation for religious objections. The Court's role is crucial in these situations, as it helps to navigate the delicate balance between the State's interest in legal investigations and the rights of religious minorities to practise their faith without undue interference.

In this regard, the ECtHR's decisions echo a broader principle: the rights of the deceased and the religious obligations of the living concerning the dead are integral to the identity and dignity of religious communities. When addressing the intersection of cultural practices and legal norms, the Court has consistently emphasised the need for a flexible approach that respects the deeply held beliefs of individuals and communities. For Muslims, the treatment of the dead and the observance of burial rituals are not just cultural practices but vital elements of their religious duty, deserving of protection under the European Convention on Human Rights.

In conclusion, the jurisprudence of the ECtHR highlights the importance of recognising and respecting the religious rights of Muslims in the handling of the dead. As legal systems evolve to address increasingly diverse societies, the principles established by the Court in cases involving Muslim religious practices, including burial and the treatment of the deceased, offer critical guidance

---

4 *Guide on Article 9 of the European Convention on Human Rights—Freedom of Thought, Conscience and Religion*, updated on 31 August 2024. Council of Europe/European Court of Human Rights, 2024, p. 55.

in ensuring that individuals' religious freedoms are upheld in a respectful and balanced manner. These cases emphasise the need for states to accommodate religious needs and cultural sensitivities, particularly in the domain of death, where respect and dignity are paramount.

Although the case law of the European Court of Human Rights regarding funerals and the handling of deceased bodies is limited, we can identify two main categories of cases. The first concerns instances in which the authorities refused to release the bodies of killed terrorists or individuals suspected of engaging in terrorist activities to their Muslim relatives. The second category addresses similar obstacles faced by relatives who were unable to receive the bodies of their loved ones for Muslim burial due to complex legal regulations and the actions of medical professionals.

1 Refusal to Release the Bodies of Terrorist Suspects to Muslim Relatives

1.1 *Sabanchiyeva and Others v. Russia* (No. 38450/05)[5]

1.1.1 Brief Overview of the Facts of the Case

This case was one of many in which relatives of terrorists killed in the Russian Federation challenged the authorities' refusal to give them the bodies of their murdered relatives for burial in accordance with the religious norms of Islam. They also stated that the authorities deliberately violated the bodies of their dead relatives (the bodies were stored without proper conditions, sometimes without clothing). In their opinion, this violated Article 8 of the Convention.

Article 8 of the European Convention on Human Rights—Right to respect for private and family life

1. Everyone has the right to respect for his private and family life, his home and his correspondence.
2. There shall be no interference by a public authority with the exercise of this right except such as is in accordance with the law and is necessary in a democratic society in the interests of national security, public safety or the economic well-being of the country, for the prevention of disorder or crime, for the protection of health or morals, or for the protection of the rights and freedoms of others.

---

5 Sabanchiyeva and Others v. Russia—38450/05—[2013] ECHR 740 (6 June 2013).

1.1.2 Position of the Court

The Court confirmed a violation of Article 8 of the Convention, but for a slightly different reason. First, it found no signs of inhumane treatment by the authorities and no intention to cause psychological suffering to the relatives of the killed, explaining this by objective logistical difficulties and the nature of the anti-terrorist operation (paragraph 112). As regards the refusal of the Russian authorities to hand over the bodies of killed terrorists, the Court stated that, in general, this measure was justified by the interests of national security in order to prevent unrest and to protect the rights and freedoms of others (paragraph 122). However, the Court did not accept the respondent Government's submission that any of the stated objectives could justify all aspects of the measure in question (paragraph 143). In particular, the Court did not, for these purposes, find a reasonable basis for completely depriving the applicants of the opportunity to participate in the relevant funeral rites or to say at least some form of goodbye to the deceased.

In fact, the Court blamed the authorities not for the failure to hand over the bodies itself, but for the failure to carry out any assessment in this regard in the present case, taking into account the individual circumstances of each of the victims and their family members (paragraph 143). The reason for this was that the applicable legislation did not consider these circumstances to be relevant, and the decision not to hand over the bodies was made purely automatically. There had thus been a violation of the applicants' right to protection of private and family life.

Some of the Judges disagreed with this decision. In their dissenting opinions, Judges Khadzhiev and Dedova stated that the Court had upset the balance between public and private interests. Since the Court had not proved that the rights to the protection of family life are more important than the right to life in general, when resolving this case it was necessary to take into account the fact that terrorists had voluntarily declared war on civilians and sowed terror among them. In such a case, terrorists usually sacrificed their bodies during attacks. In this regard, the applicants had to balance their expectations of respect for their privacy with the enormous negative consequences experienced by society as a whole.

1.2 *Gatsalova v. Russia (No. 41318/10)*[6]

1.2.1 Brief Overview of the Facts of the Case

This case is in many ways similar to the previous one, the only difference being that the applicant, the widow of a murdered Islamic terrorist, who was refused

6 Gatsalova v. Russia—41318/10 [2021] ECHR 335 (20 April 2021).

the body of her husband, additionally alleged a violation of her rights under Article 9 of the Convention.

1.2.2 Position of the Court

Since this case concerned the same anti-terrorist operation in the city of Nalchik as in *Sabanchiyeva and Others v. Russia*, the Court confirmed a violation of Article 13 of the Convention in conjunction with Article 8 in relation to the lack of effective remedies and in relation to the authorities' refusal to return the bodies of deceased relatives. However, the Court did not find a violation of Article 9 of the Convention.

Nevertheless, Judge Pavli's dissenting opinion in this case is interesting. In his view, there had also been a violation of Article 9 of the Convention. In her complaint under Article 9, the applicant had argued that the authorities' decision to cremate her husband's body instead of burying him constituted a serious interference with her freedom of religion. According to Judge Pavli, 'It is one thing not to return the body to the family; but it is another thing to dispose of the body in a manner which, according to the applicant, is incompatible with the fundamental principles of her religion' (paragraph 67 of the Dissenting opinion).

Since in the Islamic tradition (as well as in some other religions) cremation is considered to violate the dignity of the human body and is therefore strictly prohibited, Judge Pavli considered that the dismissal of the Article 9 claim was inconsistent with the Court's mandate under Article 19 of the Convention to 'ensure respect for obligations undertaken by States Parties' and to protect all fundamental rights guaranteed by the Convention.

1.2.3 Intermediate Conclusions

In conclusion, *Sabanchiyeva and Others v. Russia* and *Gatsalova v. Russia* highlight the complex intersection between the protection of individual rights and national security concerns in the context of refusing to release the bodies of terrorist suspects to their families for burial. In both cases, the applicants challenged the authorities' refusal to return the bodies of their deceased relatives, who were suspected terrorists, for Muslim burial in accordance with religious customs. The Court acknowledged the legitimate security concerns behind such refusals but emphasised that the authorities' blanket refusal to return the bodies, without considering the specific circumstances of each case or the personal needs of the families, violated those families' rights to respect for private and family life.

The Court recognised that the refusal to release the bodies was linked to national security interests, such as preventing unrest and maintaining public order. However, it concluded that these measures were not justified in a way that adequately balanced the individual rights of the family members, particularly their right to say goodbye and perform funeral rites. The Court's ruling reflects a broader human rights principle—that even in the face of serious security concerns, there should be an individualised approach to such decisions, rather than a one-size-fits-all policy.

The dissenting opinions in these cases also raised important points regarding the balance between family rights and public interests. Some judges argued that in cases involving terrorists, public safety and the protection of society should take precedence over individual family rights. These perspectives underscore the ongoing challenge in human rights jurisprudence of balancing the protection of personal freedoms with the necessity of national security measures, especially when dealing with individuals involved in terrorist activities. Overall, these cases demonstrate the need for careful consideration of both human rights and public safety when making decisions that have an impact on individuals' ability to mourn and observe cultural and religious practices.

2 Obstacles to Muslim Burials Due to Legal and mEdical Complexities

2.1 *Aygün v. Belgium (No. 28336/12)*[7]

2.1.1 Brief Overview of the Facts of the Case

The applicants' two sons were killed in September 2010, and in February 2014 a neighbour was convicted of their murders.

During the investigation, from September 2010 to April 2013, the couple was not allowed to transfer their sons' bodies to Turkey, their home country, for burial in the family grave according to their religious customs. Their challenge to this refusal in the domestic courts was unsuccessful. Before the ECtHR, they contended that the authorities' denial infringed their family and religious rights under Articles 8 and 9 of the ECHR. Additionally, they argued that they were denied an effective remedy under domestic law, in violation of Articles 6 and 13.

2.1.2 Position of the Court

The Court examined whether the interference was necessary in a democratic society (paragraph 68). It emphasised that an interference is considered 'neces-

7 Aygün v. Belgium, No. 28336/12, ECtHR (Third Section) (8 November 2022).

sary' if it addresses an 'imperative social need' and if the authorities' reasons are 'relevant and sufficient' and proportionate to the legitimate aim pursued (paragraph 69, citing *Sabanchiyeva*, § 131). In this case, the investigating judge prohibited the applicants from transferring their sons' bodies abroad until they provided proof of a burial plot in Belgium, citing the needs of the investigation (paragraph 70).

The Court reiterated that the Convention had to be interpreted as a whole, ensuring coherence between its provisions (paragraph 71). It identified competing fundamental rights: the applicants' rights under Articles 8 and 9 (respect for private and family life, and freedom of religion) versus the rights of those accused of their murder to a fair trial under Article 6 (paragraph 72). The investigation into the deaths was also subject to Article 2, which mandates an effective inquiry into suspicious deaths (paragraph 73). The Court stressed that the inquiry's effectiveness should be balanced with the applicants' rights (paragraph 74). Under the principle of subsidiarity, it is primarily for national authorities to balance competing rights, with the Court reviewing whether this balance was being maintained (paragraph 75). The interference came from a judge offering greater guarantees of independence compared to other authorities (paragraph 77). The refusal to transport the bodies was justified by the ongoing investigation and the potential impact on the case (paragraph 79). The national judge had allowed a local burial, acknowledging the applicants' religious rights but balancing them with the investigation's needs (paragraph 80).

The Court noted that the investigation was not as straightforward as the applicants suggested (paragraph 82). While the deceased were denied burial for over two years, this delay was not automatically unreasonable (paragraph 83). However, the refusal remained in place throughout the lengthy investigation, and no mechanism existed to reassess its necessity (paragraph 85). The Court found that the applicants had no way of challenging the refusal. There had therefore been a violation of Articles 8 and 9 (paragraph 91–92).

Another significant aspect of the ECtHR's jurisprudence involves the treatment of the bodies of deceased terrorists. In *Sabanchiyeva and Others v. Russia*, the Court found that the refusal to release the bodies of killed terrorists to their relatives can be acceptable under certain conditions. The Court recognised the State's interest in preventing terrorist glorification and maintaining public order. However, it also stressed the necessity of considering the individual circumstances in each case. This nuanced approach reflects the Court's commitment to balancing state security interests with the rights and dignity of individuals. Similarly, in *Gatsalova v. Russia*, the ECtHR concluded that the cremation of Muslim terrorists does not inherently violate the religious feelings of their relatives. However, the Court reiterated the importance of taking into account the specific family context. This consideration ensures that state actions are not arbitrary and that they respect the religious and cultural practices of the families involved to the greatest extent possible.

2.2 *Polat v. Austria (No. 12886/16)*[8]

2.2.1 Brief Overview of the Facts of the Case

In this case the applicants argued that their rights under Article 8 (respect for private and family life) and Article 9 (freedom of religion) of the European Convention on Human Rights had been violated.

Despite the parent applicants' religious objections to a postmortem examination, doctors at the hospital in which their child died proceeded with a full autopsy, removing all of the child's internal organs. This violated the parents' Muslim beliefs, which require the body to remain intact for ritual washing before burial. As a result, the mother experienced psychological harm, and the case was eventually brought before the Court.

The ECtHR found that the Austrian authorities had failed properly to balance public health interests with the mother's right to respect for her religious beliefs and family life, leading to a violation of both Articles 8 and 9 of the Convention.

2.2.2 Position of the Court

In this case, the Court addressed the regulation of postmortem examinations in public hospitals and whether close relatives should have the right to object to such examinations for reasons related to private life and religion when public health interests clearly call for them (paragraph 80). The case involved balancing the protection of public health through postmortem examinations and the female applicant's right to respect for her private and family life and to manifest her religion (Articles 8 and 9) (paragraph 81).

The applicant argued that her son's postmortem was not carried out properly, but the Court found that it had been conducted according to the required standards, as confirmed by an expert's opinion (paragraph 82). However, the applicant also claimed that her religious beliefs should have been considered by the hospital, and that no balancing exercise was conducted regarding her objections (paragraph 83). Austrian law did not grant an absolute right to object to a postmortem on religious or other grounds but prioritised scientific interests in cases where it was deemed necessary to do so (paragraphs 84, 85).

---

8 Polat v. Austria, No. 12886/16, ECtHR (Fourth Section) (20 July 2021).

The Court emphasised the importance of scientific advancement through postmortem examinations for public health reasons (paragraph 86). However, it also highlighted the specific sensitivity of this case, given the applicant's religious beliefs. She had informed the hospital that, according to her faith, her child's body needed to remain as unscathed as possible for the burial ceremony. The Court acknowledged that these circumstances were as sensitive as those in *Hadri-Vionnet v. Switzerland* (no. 55525/00, § 52, 14 February 2008), where the child's burial was arranged without informing the mother of the time or location. The authorities, particularly the hospital, had an increased duty to exercise a high degree of diligence and prudence in interacting with the applicant, considering the personal nature of the situation. Despite being aware of the applicant's religious objections, the hospital failed adequately to inform her about the extent of the postmortem, leading her to believe that a ritual washing and funeral ceremony could still be performed in accordance with her beliefs. This lack of transparency led the applicant to proceed with funeral arrangements in Turkey in the expectation that the body would be in an appropriate state for the ceremony (paragraphs 114, 115).

Although the Court acknowledged that the scientific interest in the postmortem was legitimate, it concluded that the authorities had not properly balanced this with the applicant's religious and family interests, particularly her wish to bury her son in accordance with her beliefs. The Supreme Court, which had addressed the scientific interests involved, gave insufficient consideration to the applicant's individual rights under Articles 8 and 9. It had failed to conduct a proper balancing exercise, which ultimately led the Court to find a violation of the applicant's rights under the Convention. The authorities had not reconciled public health interests with the applicant's rights to respect for her private and family life and to manifest her religion, thus breaching Articles 8 and 9 (paragraphs 89, 90, 91).

In their partly dissenting opinion, Judges Pastor Vilanova and Harutyunyan disagreed with the majority's refusal to examine the applicant's complaint under Article 13 of the Convention. She had objected to a postmortem examination of her deceased child on religious grounds, claiming violations of Articles 8 and 9. She had also argued that under Austrian law she had no legal right to challenge the postmortem before it took place (paragraph 1 of the dissenting opinion).

The majority decided not to address the Article 13 complaint, reasoning that the violation of Articles 8 and 9 had already been considered. However, the dissenting Judges argued that the complaint about the lack of an effective remedy was distinct and should have been examined separately, as the applicant was unable to prevent the postmortem. That operation hadcaused irreversible harm, which could not be repaired through compensation (paragraphs 3, 5–6 of the dissenting opinion).

The dissent criticised the Court's reliance on previous cases such as *Solska and Rybicka v. Poland* (Applications nos. 30491/17 and 31083/17, 20 September 2018) and *Macready v. Czech Republic* (Resolution No. CM/ResDH (2012)21, App. Nos. 4824/06, 15512/08), arguing that these cases did not sufficiently address the absence of a preventive remedy in the present case. The Judges stressed that preventive measures were essential when violations had irreversible consequences, as seen in the Court's broader case law (paragraph 8 of the dissenting opinion). They argued that the failure to provide a preventive remedy violated the applicant's rights under Article 13 and was inconsistent with the Court's preference for preventive remedies in such cases (paragraphs 9–12 of the dissenting opinion).

2.2.3 Intermediate Conclusions

In summary, *Aygün v. Belgium* and *Polat v. Austria* highlight critical issues regarding the intersection of religious rights, family life and state interests in postmortem procedures and the handling of the bodies of the deceased. In *Aygün v. Belgium*, the applicants challenged the refusal to allow them to transfer their sons' bodies for burial in accordance with their religious customs, arguing that this violated their rights under Articles 8 and 9 of the European Convention on Human Rights. The Court acknowledged the legitimate interests of the authorities in protecting the integrity of the investigation but found that the refusal was not appropriately reassessed over the course of the prolonged investigation, and no effective remedy was provided for the applicants to challenge this decision. As a result, the Court found a violation of their rights.

In *Polat v. Austria*, the Court addressed the conflict between public health interests and the applicant's religious rights when doctors conducted a postmortem on the applicant's child, despite her objections based on her faith. The Court concluded that, while the authorities had a legitimate interest in conducting the postmortem for public health reasons, they had failed adequately to consider the applicant's religious beliefs, which required the body to remain intact for burial rites. The lack of transparency and the authorities' failure to balance the public and private interests led to a violation of the applicant's rights under Articles 8 and 9.

These cases illustrate the need for a nuanced approach when balancing state interests with the protection of individual rights. They emphasise the importance of considering the specific circumstances of each case and ensuring that individuals have access to effective remedies when their fundamental rights are at stake. The rulings reflect the Court's commitment to protecting religious freedoms and family life, while also recognising the legitimate interests of the State and stressing the importance of a fair and thoughtful assessment of each situation.

CHAPTER 10

Islamic Dress

The issue of Islamic dress, particularly the wearing of the hijab and other religious garments by Muslim women, remains one of the most pressing and contentious topics in the practice of the European Court of Human Rights.[1] Legislators in Western Europe often justify bans on Muslim women wearing the hijab in public places as necessary for ensuring public safety.[2] This raises questions about a possible new form of public order, oriented towards greater social cohesion and the development of common values. The problem then hides the fact that there is a conflict between the trends of multiculturalism and calls for the assimilation of religious and national minorities in the countries party to the Convention. France, in particular, has been aggressive in trying to subordinate the Islamic value system to its secular principles, while Belgium has recently seen a relaxation of rules regarding the wearing of Muslim women's dress, France continues actively to discuss tightening these regulations even further.

The impetus for laws restricting the wearing of Muslim clothing in European countries can be traced back to reservations in international documents such as the European Convention on Human Rights and the International Covenant on Civil and Political Rights regarding the implementation of the right to freedom of religion. These documents enshrine that right but also allow for its restriction under certain circumstances.[3] However, the permissibility of restricting immutable human rights is not always unanimously interpreted at the legislative level. In particular, often, the grounds and scope of restrictions at the national level are judged not to be aligned with the spirit of international acts, which are fundamentally interpreted as an extensive protection and sup-

1 See Durham, W. Cole, ed., *Islam, Europe and Emerging Legal Issues* (Farnham: Ashgate Publishing, 2012).

2 Nanwani, Shaira, 'The Burqa Ban: An Unreasonable Limitation on Religious Freedom or a Justifiable Restriction?', *Emory International Law Review* 25 (2011), p. 1431.

3 About this see Evans, Carolyn, 'The Islamic Scarf in the European Court of Human Rights,' *Melbourne Journal of International Law* 7 (2006), p. 52; Baderin, Mashood, 'Islamic Law and the Implementation of Human Rights Law: A Case Study of the International Covenant on Civil and Political Rights,' in Baderin, Mashood, and Ssenyonjo, Manisuli, eds., *International Human Rights Law: Six Decades after the UDHR and Beyond* (Aldershot: Ashgate, 2010), pp. 337–357.

port of human rights. This misalignment frequently results in conflicts between state and supra-national jurisdictions.

In this regard, the practice of the ECtHR regarding the wearing of religious clothing and symbols is highly contradictory and frequently criticised. In some cases, the European Court justifies the ban on wearing religious clothing, while in others it permits it. This inconsistency reflects the tension between a specific national tradition of secularism and the desire of the supra-national Court to balance religious equality and neutrality-non-discrimination. For instance, the Court has approved various prohibitions on the use of religious symbols in the interests of secularism. However, there are signs that it is becoming more attentive to the feelings of believers and the cultural and historical characteristics of particular countries.

To understand this issue better, this section is divided into two parts: the wearing of Islamic clothing in public spaces and the wearing of Islamic clothing by public servants whose professions, in some national contexts, impose certain restrictions on their religious expression.

The ECtHR has ruled on several cases involving bans on Islamic dress in public spaces. In these cases, the Court often upholds national laws, citing the margin of appreciation that states enjoy in balancing individual rights against collective interests. The margin of appreciation doctrine allows states a degree of discretion in how they implement human rights obligations, recognising that national authorities are better positioned to assess local needs and conditions.

However, critics argue that such rulings undermine the fundamental right to freedom of religion and expression.[4] They contend that these bans disproportionately target Muslim women and contribute to their discrimination, marginalisation and exclusion from public life. Furthermore, the bans are seen as infringing the personal autonomy and dignity of Muslim women who choose to wear the hijab or other religious garments as an expression of their faith.

The issue of Islamic dress becomes even more complex when it involves public servants whose professions impose certain restrictions on their religious expression. For instance, teachers, police officers and other public employees are often required to maintain religious neutrality in the workplace. This requirement is particularly strong in legal systems that adopted an interpretation of secularism inspired by the French *laïcité*.

4 McCrea, Ronan, 'The Ban on the Veil and European Law,' *Human Rights Law Review* 13, no. 1 (March 2013), pp. 57–97.

The ECtHR has ruled on cases involving public servants who have been prohibited from wearing religious symbols, including Islamic dress, while on duty. In these cases, the Court has generally supported the restrictions, emphasising the need to maintain public confidence in the neutrality and impartiality of public institutions. However, it has also recognised the importance of protecting individual religious freedoms and has called for a careful balancing of competing interests.

The ECtHR's approach underscores the importance of context in adjudicating on cases involving religious dress. The Court must navigate the complex interplay of national laws, cultural traditions and individual rights, often with no easy answers. As Europe continues to grapple with issues of religious diversity and secularism, the ECtHR's jurisprudence will play a critical role in shaping the future of religious freedoms for Muslims and other religious minorities.

1 Dress Code in the Public Space

1.1 *Lachiri v. Belgium (No. 3413/09)*[5]

1.1.1 Brief Overview of the Facts of the Case

The applicant and members of her family were involved in a court case seeking damages in connection with the murder of her brother. On the day of the hearing at the indictment chamber of the Brussels Court of Appeal, in accordance with the decision of the presiding judge, the court reporter told the applicant that she would not be able to enter the courtroom until she removed her hijab. The applicant refused to comply and did not attend the hearing. Relying on Article 9 (right to freedom of thought, conscience and religion), she complained that her exclusion from the courtroom violated her freedom to express her religion.

1.1.2 Position of the Court

The Court found a violation of Article 9 of the Convention. It noted that it appeared from the case file that, in order to exclude the applicant from the courtroom, the President of the Indictment Chamber had simply referred to a provision of law which, according to her interpretation, prohibited the applicant from wearing the Islamic hijab. Then the Prosecution Chamber based its decision in this matter solely on the fact that the contested measure was in accordance with the law (paragraph 43).

---

5 Lachiri v. Belgium—3413/09 French Text [2018] ECHR 727 (18 September 2018).

The Court also noted that it was effectively a 'public' institution in which respect for neutrality of belief might take precedence over the free exercise of the right to manifest one's religion, in like manner to public educational institutions (paragraph 45). However, since it did not follow from the procedural documents that the applicant was excluded in order to maintain such neutrality, and there were no other violations on her part, there has been a violation of Article 9 of the Convention.

The Judges disagreed with this decision of the court and considered it necessary to speak out about the case under consideration. Judges Vucinic and Gritsko expressed the opinion that the court should have concentrated on the legislative provision on the basis of which the applicant was not allowed to attend the hearing. It followed from the circumstances of the case that its provisions (Article 759 of the Belgian Judicial Code), as formulated, did not in themselves create any problems under Article 9 of the Convention (paragraphs 26–27). Thus, the violation of Article 9 resulted from an incorrect interpretation of procedural law.

Judge Mura-Wikström dissented from the majority opinion. He noted that simply attending a hearing as a spectator was not comparable to participating as a party to a lawsuit. According to Judge Moore-Wikström, the judicial 'ritual' of which clothing is a component aimed to erase the personal differences of each person in order to place legal and judicial debate at the centre of the trial. The protection of this order serves the proper functioning of state institutions.

Accordingly, in the view of the dissenting minority of Judges, the applicant's wish to wear the hijab in this case could not be protected by Article 9 of the Convention.

1.2 *S.A.S. v. France (No. 43835/11)*[6]

1.2.1 Brief Overview of the Facts of the Case

The decision in *S.A.S. v. France* precipitated a multifaceted discourse concerning the intersection of religious freedom, cultural diversity, and state neutrality within the European legal landscape. The decision emphasised the ECtHR's pivotal role in delineating the contours of permissible restrictions on fundamental rights, particularly in contexts fraught with complex socio-cultural dynamics and competing normative paradigms.

In *S.A.S. v. France* (Application No. 43835/11) before the European Court of Human Rights, the central contention revolved around the compatibility of

6 S.A.S. v. France—43835/11—Grand Chamber Judgment [2014] ECHR 695 (1 July 2014).

France's legislative prohibition on the wearing of full-face veils, notably the niqab and burqa, in public spaces, with the provisions of the European Convention on Human Rights (paragraph 1). The applicant, identified as S.A.S., advanced the argument that the ban contravened her rights enshrined under Articles 8 (right to respect for private and family life), 9 (freedom of thought, conscience, and religion), 10 (freedom of expression) and 14 (prohibition of discrimination) of the ECtHR (paragraph 2).

As a result of the ban, S.A.S. was subject to potential fines or other penalties if she chose to continue wearing the niqab in violation of the law. Therefore, the ban directly impacted on her ability to exercise her religious beliefs and cultural practices in accordance with her convictions.

1.2.2 Position of the Court

The Court did not find a violation of the Convention. In its deliberation, it conducted an assessment of the impugned legislation in light of the principles articulated within the ECtHR framework (paragraph 56). It acknowledged the State's prerogative in imposing restrictions on individual rights within the limitations of Article 9(2) of the Convention, provided that such limitations were prescribed by law and necessary in a democratic society (paragraph 120). Emphasising the margin of appreciation accorded to member states in adjudicating on matters touching upon religious practices and societal norms (paragraph 121), the ECtHR determined that France's prohibition on full-face veils pursued legitimate objectives, notably the promotion of social cohesion, gender equality and the protection of public safety and order (paragraph 122).

Furthermore, the Court stressed the State's discretion in assessing the balance between competing rights and interests, highlighting the nuanced considerations inherent in reconciling religious manifestations with broader societal values and norms (paragraph 123). Despite acknowledging the importance of individual autonomy and religious freedom, the ECtHR ultimately upheld the impugned ban, reasoning that it constituted a proportionate response to the State's legitimate aims, while also preserving the rights and freedoms of others (paragraph 145).

In their joint partly dissenting opinion in *S.A.S. v. France* (No. 43835/11), Judges Nussberger and Jäderblom expressed reservations regarding the majority's decision on the compatibility of France's ban on the wearing of full-face veils (such as the niqab and burqa) in public spaces with the European Convention on Human Rights.

The Judges acknowledged the importance of the State's interest in promoting social cohesion, gender equality and public safety, which were cited by France as justifications for the ban. However, they debated that the blanket ban on the full-face veil disproportionately restricted the rights of individuals to manifest their religious beliefs under Article 9 (freedom of thought, conscience, and religion) of the ECtHR.

Judges Nussberger and Jäderblom emphasised that any limitations on religious freedoms must be proportionate to the legitimate aims pursued by the State. They noted that a complete ban on the full-face veil was a particularly severe interference with religious freedom and that less restrictive measures could have been considered to achieve the State's objectives.

Furthermore, the Judges expressed concerns about the potential stigmatisation and marginalisation of Muslim women who choose to wear the full-face veil. They argue that such a ban could exacerbate social tensions and discrimination against Muslim communities rather than promoting integration and social cohesion.

Overall, while Judges Nussberger and Jäderblom acknowledged the State's legitimate aims, they believed that the blanket ban on the full-face veil disproportionately interfered with individuals' rights to freedom of religion and could have negative societal implications. Therefore, they partially dissented from the majority's decision, advocating for a more nuanced approach to balancing religious freedoms and societal interests.

1.3 *Dakir v. Belgium (No. 4619/12)*[7]

1.3.1 Brief Overview of the Facts of the Case

In *Dakir v. Belgium* (Application No. 4619/12), the applicant, Ms. Dakir, was a Muslim woman residing in Belgium. The case arose from an incident in which Ms. Dakir was required to remove her headscarf, a religious garment commonly worn by Muslim women, in order to enter a courtroom and participate in legal proceedings.

Belgium had a legal requirement that individuals had to remove head coverings, including religious headscarves, when entering courtrooms. This requirement was enforced as part of courtroom decorum regulations aimed at maintaining neutrality and impartiality within the judicial system.

Ms. Dakir argued that Belgium's requirement violated her rights under the European Convention on Human Rights, specifically Articles 8 (right to respect for private and family life), 9 (freedom of thought, conscience, and religion), and 14 (prohibition of discrimination).

---

7 Dakir v. Belgium—4619/12 French Text [2017] ECHR 656 (11 July 2017).

1.3.2 Position of the Court

The Court did not find a violation of Article 8, 9 or 14 of the Convention. Despite acknowledging the significance of religious freedom and the importance of upholding individual rights, the Court determined that Belgium's requirement for Ms. Dakir to remove her headscarf in order to access justice was within the margin of appreciation afforded to member states.

The ECtHR recognised Belgium's legitimate aim of ensuring the proper functioning of the judicial process and maintaining courtroom decorum and impartiality. The Court concluded that the restriction on religious attire, while impacting on Ms. Dakir's religious practice, was proportionate to the legitimate aims pursued by Belgium.

Judge Spano and Judge Karakas acknowledged Belgium's legitimate aim of ensuring the proper functioning of the judicial process and maintaining courtroom decorum. They recognised the State's discretion in regulating certain aspects of public life, including courtroom procedures, and the importance of upholding the principle of secularism in the administration of justice.

However, the Judges emphasised the need for proportionality and respect for individual rights, particularly the freedom of religion, guaranteed under Article 9 of the ECtHR. They noted that while States have a margin of appreciation in matters of religion, such discretion is not unlimited, and restrictions on religious attire must be carefully balanced against the rights of individuals.

1.4 *Hamidović c. Bosnia-Herzegovine (No. 57792/15)*[8]

1.4.1 Brief Overview of the Facts of the Case

This case concerned the ban on wearing a religious Islamic head covering in court. Of course, it could have been considered on a par with *Dakir v. Belgium* (No. 4619/12) and *Lachiri v. Belgium* (No. 3413/09). However, in my opinion, the present case is distinguished by the fact that the applicant was brought into criminal proceedings against his will and suffered a significantly more severe punishment in the form of imprisonment. Also in the present case, the Court found a violation of Article 9 of the Convention, which was not the case in similar cases regarding the ban on wearing the hijab.

In this case, the applicant, while a witness in a criminal trial against members of his religious organisation, refused to remove his headdress, a skullcap, for religious reasons when ordered to by the court. For this, he was sentenced to a fine for contempt of court and, after refusing to pay this fine, to a month in

8 Hamidović c. Bosnia-Herzegovina—57792/15 [2017] ECHR 1101 (5 December 2017).

prison. The applicant considered that the authorities' actions violated Article 9 of the Convention.

1.4.2 Position of the Court

The Court found that there had been a violation of Article 9 of the Convention. It noted at the outset that the applicant had no choice but to appear before a national court: under the Code of Criminal Procedure of Bosnia and Herzegovina, a witness's failure to appear risked a fine or arrest (paragraph 37). The Court also indicated that the applicant had not committed any other actions indicating contempt of court, and his religious motives were sincere (paragraph 41).

The Court considered that the interference with the applicant's rights was excessive and unjustified, at least because he was a private person (paragraph 40). Moreover, given that he, unlike some other members of his religious group (paragraph 6), appeared before the court when summoned and stood up when asked, thereby clearly obeying the laws and courts of the land, his punishment was not necessary in a democratic society. In this case, the national authorities exceeded the wide margin of appreciation granted to them and there was a violation of Article 9 of the Convention.

Some of the Judges considered it necessary to comment on the present case. Judge de Gaetano, in a separate opinion, noted that although this case was entirely concerned with freedom of religious expression, the applicant had been punished on the basis of a general and vague provision of law, which the domestic courts had ignored.

Judge Bosniak supported this opinion emphasising that discretion should be exercised by democratically legitimate authorities rather than by individual entities. Unlike cases with general rules prohibiting religious symbols, here the Judge established a ban without such a rule, which influenced its necessity. The applicant's insubordination amounted to conscientious objection rather than contempt of court. In addition, the Judge was unable to justify how the skullcap could interfere with the trial.

The last to speak was Judge Ranzoni, who considered that there had been no violation of Article 9 of the Convention. The Judge emphasised the importance of secularism in Bosnia and Herzegovina and argued that the decisions of the domestic courts were well reasoned and within the margin of appreciation. He questions the majority's analysis, especially regarding the lack of European consensus and the lack of a nuanced approach to balancing conflicting rights.

1.4.3 Intermediate Conclusions

The European Court of Human Rights generally supports secular legislators' restrictions on wearing Muslim religious headdresses in public places. This approach, however, is not without controversy among the judges. For instance, in *S.A.S. v. France*, the applicant challenged France's ban on wearing full-face veils in public spaces. The Court acknowledged that the ban interfered with the applicant's right to manifest her religion. However, it concluded that the interference was justified by the State's interest in ensuring public safety and social cohesion. The Court found that the ban aimed to promote 'living together' and that the measure was proportionate to the aims pursued. Similarly, in *Dakir v. Belgium*, the Court upheld Belgium's ban on full-face veils. It reiterated its reasoning in the *S.A.S.* case, emphasising that the ban pursued legitimate aims such as ensuring public safety and protecting the rights and freedoms of others. The Court held that the measure was necessary in a democratic society and thus did not violate the applicant's rights under the Convention.

While the ECtHR typically supports restrictions on Islamic dress in public spaces, it made a notable exception in *Lachiri v. Belgium*. In this case, the applicant was excluded from a courtroom for wearing a hijab. The Court acknowledged that, like universities, courts are public institutions where the neutrality of belief can be prioritised over the free exercise of religious expression. However, the Court found that in this instance the applicant's exclusion was not justified. It noted that the courtroom had not explicitly declared its neutrality in matters of religious expression. Therefore, the applicant's exclusion for wearing a hijab could not be considered contempt of court. The Court held that there were no other signs of disrespect, and the exclusion was a disproportionate interference with her right to manifest her religion. This decision highlighted the importance of context and the specific circumstances of each case when determining the permissibility of restrictions on religious dress.

Another critical aspect of the ECtHR's approach is the protection of religious attire, particularly in judicial settings. In *Hamidović v. Bosnia-Herzegovina*, the Court addressed the prosecution of an individual who refused to remove his religious headdress during a criminal trial. The ECtHR found that prosecuting someone for adhering to their religious dress code during court proceedings was unacceptable, as it violated their right to religious freedom under Article 9 of the Convention. This case highlighted the Court's commitment to ensuring that individuals are not forced to choose between their religious beliefs and participating in legal processes.

The ECtHR's decisions on Islamic dress in public spaces have far-reaching implications and are often controversial. The Court's general stance of upholding bans is based on the principles of secularism and the State's interest in maintaining public order and security. However, these rulings are frequently met with dissenting opinions from the judges who argue that such restrictions disproportionately impact on the religious rights of Muslim women. The controversies and dissenting opinions among the judges reveal the need for a careful and nuanced consideration of the impact of such restrictions on the rights of Muslim individuals. As societal attitudes and legal frameworks evolve, the ECtHR's role in interpreting and balancing these competing interests remains crucial.

2 Islamic Dress and Public Service

2.1 *Dahlab v. Switzerland (No. 42393/98)*[9]

Brief overview of the circumstances of the case

In *Dahlab v. Switzerland* (No. 42393/98), the European Court of Human Rights addressed the dismissal of a Swiss public-school teacher, Mrs. Dahlab, who refused to remove her Islamic headscarf (hijab) during classroom instruction. Mrs. Dahlab stated that wearing the hijab was an expression of her religious beliefs and that her dismissal amounted to discrimination based on her religion.

Switzerland justified Mrs. Dahlab's dismissal by invoking the principle of secularism in public education, asserting that allowing her to wear the hijab could compromise the neutrality and secular nature of education in the country. The applicant complained of a violation of Article 9 of the Convention.

2.1.1 Position of the Court

The Court rejected the complaint. The ECtHR acknowledged the importance of secularism in public education but emphasised that the right to manifest one's religion is protected under the European Convention on Human Rights, specifically Article 9 (freedom of thought, conscience, and religion) (paragraph 38). However, it noted that States have a wide margin of appreciation in educational matters and that Switzerland's aim of preserving secularism in schools was legitimate.

In its decision, the ECtHR concluded that Switzerland had not violated Mrs. Dahlab's rights under the Convention. It found that the Swiss authorities had not acted arbitrarily or disproportionately in dismissing Mrs. Dahlab (paragraph 39). It was held that Switzerland's restrictions on religious attire in public school classrooms were within the State's margin of appreciation and did not unduly infringe Mrs. Dahlab's freedom of religion (paragraph 41).

---

9 Dahlab v. Switzerland—42393/98 [2001] ECHR 899 (15 February 2001).

Therefore, the ECtHR ruled that there had been no violation of the European Convention on Human Rights in *Dahlab v. Switzerland* (No. 42393/98) (paragraph 41). The decision underlines the importance of balancing religious freedoms with the legitimate aims of secularism and neutrality in public education systems.

So, the prohibition imposed on a public elementary school teacher on wearing a headscarf did not breach Article 9 of the ECtHR.

2.2 *Kurtulmus v. Turkey (No. 65500/01)*[10]

2.2.1 Brief Overview of the Facts of the Case

The applicant, a university lecturer, was prohibited by the university authorities from wearing the hijab during lectures, this view being based on the Turkish principle of secularism. The applicant argued that this violated a number of provisions of the Convention, in particular Articles 6, 7, 8, 9 and 10 and Article 1 of Protocol No. 1.

Article 1 of Protocol 1 to the European Convention on Human Rights—Protection of property

Every natural or legal person is entitled to the peaceful enjoyment of his possessions. No one shall be deprived of his possessions except in the public interest and subject to the conditions provided for by law and by the general principles of international law.
The preceding provisions shall not, however, in any way impair the right of a State to enforce such laws as it deems necessary to control the use of property in accordance with the general interest or to secure the payment of taxes or other contributions or penalties.

2.2.2 Position of the Court

The Court found the complaint inadmissible. It noted that in a democratic society the State had the right to restrict the wearing of Islamic headscarves if this practice was contrary to the purpose of protecting the rights and freedoms of others. In this case, the applicant decided to become a government employee. The dress code in question, which applied without distinction to all employees of the civil service, was intended to support the principles of secularism and neutrality of the civil service and, in particular, public education. Moreover, the extent of such measures and the mechanisms for their implementation

10 Kurtulmus v. Turkey—65500/01 [2006] ECHR 1169 (24 January 2006).

must inevitably remain to some extent at the discretion of the State concerned. Consequently, having regard to the margin of appreciation enjoyed by the Contracting States in this matter, the interference complained of was in principle justified and proportionate.

The Court also noted that the rules regarding the wearing of the Islamic hijab are not related to the applicant's religion or womanhood, but have, in particular, the legitimate aim of protecting order and the rights and freedoms of others and are clearly intended to preserve the secular nature of educational institutions and the resulting principle of neutrality of the civil service.

This part of the application therefore had to be rejected as manifestly ill-founded within the meaning of Article 35(3) and (4) of the Convention.

2.3 *Ebrahimian v. France (No. 64846/11)*[11]

2.3.1 Brief Overview of the Facts of the Case

The applicant, Ms. Ebrahimian, was employed as a hospital nurse in a public hospital in France. The hospital had a dress code that prohibited employees from wearing conspicuous religious symbols while on duty. Ms. Ebrahimian, a Muslim woman, wore a hijab as part of her religious observance.

When Ms. Ebrahimian's employment contract came up for renewal, the hospital management informed her that it would not be renewed unless she agreed to remove her hijab while at work, in accordance with the hospital's dress code. Ms. Ebrahimian refused to comply with this request, citing her religious beliefs and arguing that wearing the hijab was an essential aspect of her identity and religious practice.

As a result of her refusal to remove her hijab, the hospital decided not to renew Ms. Ebrahimian's employment contract. In response, Ms. Ebrahimian brought a complaint before the European Court of Human Rights, alleging a violation of her rights under Article 9 (freedom of thought, conscience, and religion) of the European Convention on Human Rights.

2.3.2 Position of the Court

The Court rejected the applicant's complaint. First, it recalled that States could invoke the principle of secularism and state neutrality to justify restrictions on the wearing of religious symbols by public servants, in particular teachers working in public institutions (paragraph 57). Civil servants were distinguished from other citizens by their status as public representatives (paragraph 64).

---

11 Ebrahimian v. France—64846/11 [2015] ECHR 1041 (26 November 2015).

The Court noted that the hospital management had appropriately emphasised that the requisite neutrality requirement was mandatory, given the contacts it had with patients (paragraph 69). Moreover, the applicant was aware of the existing legal requirements for the clothing of employees of government agencies (paragraph 70). The administration reminded her of this and asked her to reconsider the decision to wear the hijab. It was because of her refusal to comply with this obligation that the applicant was notified of the commencement of disciplinary proceedings, regardless of her professional qualities.

Accordingly, the Court concluded that the interference with the applicant's freedom to manifest her religion was necessary in a democratic society and there was no violation of Article 9 of the Convention.

Judge O'Leary issued a partly concurring and partly dissenting opinion. While she agreed with the majority's finding that the refusal to renew Ms. Ebrahimian's employment contract did not violate Article 9 of the European Convention on Human Rights, she expressed concerns about the proportionality of the restriction on wearing religious symbols. Judge O'Leary called for a more thorough assessment of the specific circumstances and alternative measures to balance religious freedom with the hospital's objectives of maintaining neutrality and secularism.

Judge Goetano agreed with Judge O Leary's opinion. He called for greater attention to individual cases, pointing out as an example that a woman may wear a headscarf not to demonstrate religious belief or any other belief, but for several reasons. Thus, it was very important to establish the reason why a civil servant wore a particular item of clothing that did not comply with the requirements.

2.3.3 Intermediate Conclusions

The European Court of Human Rights' position is consistent: the wearing of Muslim religious clothing by public service employees is generally unacceptable due to the requirements of secularism, religious neutrality and the special obligations placed on civil servants. This stance emphasises the need for public employees to be aware of these requirements when entering into employment contracts. While personal religious freedoms are protected under the European Convention on Human Rights, the Court has emphasised that these freedoms can be restricted in public service to ensure adherence to broader societal values, such as neutrality and secularism. However, it is important to note that the Court's decisions do not universally ban the wearing of religious dress or symbols in public office across all member states. Instead, it allows each country to exercise its margin of appreciation, meaning that decisions on this issue are specific to the individual countries and their unique legal and cultural contexts.

The principle of secularism and religious neutrality underpins many of the ECtHR's rulings regarding Islamic dress in public service. Secularism in this context is understood as the separation of religious institutions from state institutions and ensuring that public service remains neutral in religious matters. This neutrality is crucial for maintaining the impartiality and equality that public institutions are expected to uphold.

The ECtHR has also highlighted the specific requirements and obligations that come with public service positions. Employees of public institutions are expected to uphold the principles of neutrality and impartiality, which can necessitate restrictions on religious expressions, including the wearing of Islamic dress.

In *Kurtulmus v. Turkey*, a university lecturer challenged the prohibition on wearing a hijab while teaching at a public university. The Turkish authorities maintained that the ban was necessary to ensure the secular nature of the university and to prevent any potential influence on students. The ECtHR sided with the authorities, stating that public employees, particularly those in educational roles, had to adhere to the principles of secularism and religious neutrality. The Court reiterated that these principles were crucial to maintaining public trust in the impartiality of state institutions.

Similarly, in *Ebrahimian v. France*, the case involved a social worker in a public hospital who was dismissed for refusing to remove her hijab. The French authorities justified the dismissal by citing the need to uphold secularism and religious neutrality within public services, especially in healthcare settings where patients might have diverse religious beliefs. The ECtHR upheld the dismissal, emphasising that the requirement for public employees to maintain neutrality justified the restriction on religious dress. The Court pointed out that these requirements were clear, and that the applicant was aware of them when entering into her employment contract.

This approach ensures that public institutions remain spaces in which individuals from diverse backgrounds feel equally respected and that the public's trust in these institutions' impartiality is preserved. The Court's decisions indicate that while personal religious freedoms are protected under the European Convention on Human Rights, these freedoms can legitimately be restricted in the context of public service to uphold broader societal values.

CHAPTER 11

Protection of Religious Beliefs: Criteria for Islamophobia

Despite abundant literature on Islamophobia, a universally accepted definition remains elusive.[1] At its core, Islamophobia encompasses prejudice against Muslims, translating into intolerant attitudes that manifest themselves as discriminatory policies and practices targeting Muslims. The European Court of Human Rights plays a pivotal role in addressing these issues, balancing the right to freedom of expression with the principle of non-discrimination and respect for religious diversity.

The right to freedom of expression is a fundamental tenet in democratic societies. However, it does not grant *carte blanche* to make critical or disparaging statements about any religion or religious practices. International legal instruments, including the European Convention on Human Rights, articulate the contradiction inherent in this principle. They prohibit any propaganda regarding national, racial or religious hatred that incites discrimination, hostility or violence.[2]

Islamophobia often manifests itself through targeted hate crimes and discriminatory behaviours aimed at Muslims or those perceived to be Muslim. Such acts of violence or hostility are frequently motivated by negative stereotypes about Islam, with perpetrators linking Muslims to terrorism, extremism or other negative attributes. These stereotypes may be further compounded by high-profile incidents or media portrayals that connect Muslims to acts of violence or radicalism, fostering a climate of suspicion and fear.

According to the Guidelines of the OSCE Office for Democratic Institutions and Human Rights (ODIHR), the Council of Europe and UNESCO on 'Understanding Anti-Muslim Hate Crimes'. 'anti-Muslim prejudice is a bias motivation that turns a criminal offense into a hate crime. An anti-Muslim hate crime is

1 See, e.g., Bleich, Erik, 'Defining and Researching Islamophobia,' *Review of Middle East Studies* 46.2 (2012), pp. 180–189; Bravo López, Fernando, 'Towards a Definition of Islamophobia: Approximations of the Early Twentieth Century,' *Ethnic and Racial Studies* 34.4 (2011), pp. 556–573.

2 European Parliament. *Resolution on the Right to Freedom of Expression and Respect for Religious Beliefs*, Resolution 1510 (2006). Parliamentary Assembly, 28 June 2006. https://assembly.coe.int/nw/xml/XRef/Xref-XML2HTML-en.asp?fileid=17457.

established when it is evident that the perpetrator selected the victim based on their Islamic faith or perceived association with Islam.'[3] These crimes are targeted not only at Muslims but also at individuals perceived as Muslim or associated with Muslims, including non-Muslim spouses, allies or even individuals from communities such as the Sikhs, who may be mistaken for Muslims. This highlights the broader scope of Islamophobic violence, which can affect a range of individuals linked to Islam in various ways.

While hate crimes against Muslims are frequently directed at individuals, they can also target institutions or properties associated with Islam. Islamic centres, mosques and organisations that provide services to Muslim communities, such as those offering support or training for Muslim women or youth, are also frequently targets of violence and vandalism. Acts of hate against these institutions may include the desecration of religious spaces, vandalising property, or anti-Muslim graffiti, further contributing to an atmosphere of fear and division.

These forms of Islamophobic violence are not limited to physical assaults but can also include subtle forms of abuse, such as verbal insults or exclusion from social, educational or professional spaces. It is important to recognise that these acts often blend religious prejudice with ethnic and racial discrimination, as perpetrators may target individuals based on their appearance, clothing or names, associating them with Islam. This intersection of religious, ethnic and racial biases amplifies the marginalisation of Muslims and creates barriers to their full participation in society.

In educational settings, for instance, Muslim students may face exclusion due to their religious practices, such as wearing a hijab, which can exacerbate feelings of alienation and negatively affect their mental and emotional wellbeing. In the workplace, Muslim employees may encounter discrimination through biased treatment or through being overlooked for opportunities. These forms of Islamophobia contribute not only to the harm faced by individual victims but also to broader societal divisions, undermining social cohesion and hindering efforts for integration and mutual understanding.

As highlighted in the ODIHR guidelines, addressing Islamophobia requires comprehensive legal measures to restrain and/or punish offenders while also tackling the underlying prejudices that sustain such hate crimes. Moreover, societal initiatives are necessary to challenge and dismantle the stereotypes

---

3 *Understanding Anti-Muslim Hate Crimes: Addressing the Security Needs of Muslim Communities: A Practical Guide* (Warsaw: OSCE Office for Democratic Institutions and Human Rights, 2020),pp. 8–9.

and misconceptions that perpetuate discrimination, fostering a more inclusive environment for Muslims and non-Muslims alike.

This tension is particularly evident in cases of Islamophobia. The ECtHR's jurisprudence often navigates these delicate waters, ensuring that freedom of expression does not encroach upon the rights of individuals to be free from hate speech and discrimination based on their religious beliefs.

Islamophobia, in the context of the ECtHR, is examined through cases involving insults based on religious affiliation and discrimination rooted in Islamic religious practices. These cases illuminate the complexities of Islamophobia and the legal intricacies involved in addressing it.

Cases involving insults based on religious affiliation often test the limits of freedom of expression. The ECtHR has established that while freedom of expression is crucial, it is not absolute. It must be weighed against the potential harm caused by hate speech. The Court examines whether the statements in question incite hatred or violence against Muslims or whether they merely constitute critical discourse within the bounds of acceptable debate.

For instance, the Court considers the context in which statements are made, the intent behind them, and their potential impact on public order and the rights of others. Statements that unequivocally incite violence or hatred are not protected under the guise of freedom of expression. The ECtHR strives to ensure that public discourse remains open and free, yet respectful of the dignity and rights of all individuals, including Muslims.

Discrimination cases often revolve around practices integral to the Islamic faith, such as wearing religious attire, observing dietary laws or accessing religious education. The ECtHR assesses whether restrictions on these practices are justified within the framework of the European Convention on Human Rights.

The Court examines whether the restrictions serve a legitimate aim, such as public safety, health or order, and whether they are proportionate to the intended aim. The principle of proportionality is crucial in these assessments. The ECtHR evaluates whether the restrictive measures are the least intrusive means of achieving the legitimate aim and whether they disproportionately burden the individual's religious freedoms.

The phenomenon of Islamophobia is multifaceted, involving prejudice, intolerance and discrimination against Muslims. The ECtHR's approach to addressing Islamophobia reflects this complexity, balancing competing rights and interests within the framework of the European Convention on Human Rights.

The legal features of Islamophobia cases before the ECtHR involve careful consideration of several factors. These include the context and intent of the actions or statements in question, the potential harm to individuals and society, and the broader implications for human rights and public order. In cases of insults based on religious affiliation, the Court evaluates whether the statements constitute hate speech or legitimate criticism. It considers the potential for such statements to incite violence or hatred and their impact on social cohesion and public order. In discrimination cases, the ECtHR examines whether the restrictions on religious practices are justified by legitimate aims and are proportionate to those aims. The Court ensures that measures do not disproportionately burden the religious freedoms of Muslims and that they align with the principles of non-discrimination and respect for diversity.

1 Offences against Religious Beliefs

1.1 *E.S. v. Austria (No. 38450/12)*[4]

1.1.1 Brief Overview of the Facts of the Case

The applicant conducted several seminars entitled 'Basic Information on Islam' at the Educational Institute of the right-wing Freedom Party. Several statements she made during these (public) seminars were directed against the doctrines of Islam, which essentially conveyed the message that Muhammad had paedophile tendencies. She was found guilty of disregard for religious doctrines under Article 188 of the Criminal Code. The Austrian courts found her guilty of publicly humiliating the object of veneration of the domestic church or religious society, namely Muhammad, the Prophet of Islam, in a manner capable of causing justifiable indignation. The applicant considered that this had violated Article 10 of the Convention.

1.1.2 Position of the Court

The Court held that there had been no violation of Article 10 of the Convention. It emphasised that the applicant's offensive remarks about the Prophet Muhammad were made within a broader context. While acknowledging the provocative nature of her statements and their potential to offend Muslims, the Court underscored the importance of considering the context in which these remarks were delivered (paragraph 50).

Austrian courts conducted a detailed analysis of the seminars in which the applicant made these statements, taking into account factors such as the timing, setting and audience for the events (51–53). They recognised that, as a

4 E.S. v. Austria—38450/12 [2018] ECHR 891 (25 October 2018).

seminar speaker, the applicant held a position of influence over her audience, amplifying the impact of her words (paragraph 53).

In the Court's view, the domestic courts' decisions reflect a careful balance between the EU's right to freedom of expression and the State's duty to prevent sectarian tensions and protect religious harmony (paragraphs 54–55). Thus, in the Court's view, it was incompatible with Article 10 of the Convention to package incriminating statements in the guise of an otherwise acceptable expression of opinion.

Thus, the European Court of Human Rights concluded that while the applicant's remarks may have been offensive, they were made within a broader context that was carefully evaluated by the Austrian courts (paragraphs 57–58). Moreover, in the Court's view, the applicant was given a small fine, which demonstrated the moderation of the decisions of the national courts (paragraph 56). Consequently, the Court found no violation of the applicant's right to freedom of expression under Article 10 of the European Convention on Human Rights.

1.2 *Sanchez v. France (No. 45581/15)*[5]

1.2.1 Brief Overview of the Facts of the Case

The case concerned online incitement to racial hatred or violence against people of the Muslim faith. The applicant, a locally elected official and legislative candidate for a far-right party, was convicted by French courts of inciting hatred against a group or person on the basis of a particular religion, and of failing promptly to remove third parties' posting of controversial comments on his Facebook wall. The complaint was based on Article 10 of the Convention.

1.2.2 Position of the Court

The Court did not find an alleged violation of Article 10 of the Convention. It emphasised that politicians have a responsibility to avoid comments that may promote intolerance, especially during public speeches (paragraph 150). The Court also drew attention to the risks of hate speech on the Internet and recognised the possibility of legal liability (paragraph 185). In the context of a case in which controversial comments were published on behalf of a politician on his Facebook page in the run-up to the elections, the Court found these statements to be illegal. He also emphasised that politicians bear a special burden of responsibility for the use of social media, given their wide audience

5 Sanchez v. France—45581/15 [2023] ECHR 418 (15 May 2023).

(paragraph 176). Despite the applicant's objections that it was unreasonable to prosecute him instead of the authors of the comments, the Court did not find a violation of the law and noted that the applicant was unable to prove the arbitrariness of the State's actions (paragraphs 182–189).

In the present case, the Court noted that imposing a prison sentence for a violation of the offence of political speech may be compatible with the freedom of expression guaranteed by Article 10 of the Convention, but only in exceptional circumstances (paragraph 207). Since the applicant was given a fine significantly less than that for the upper limit of the criminal offence under which the proceedings were brought against him, and this had no impact on his political career, the Court considered that the impugned interference could be considered 'necessary in a democratic society'. Accordingly, there was no violation of Article 10 of the Convention.

In his dissenting opinion, Judge Ravarani argued that while he agreed with much of the Court's reasoning, he could not vote for the operative part of the decision. In this respect, he noted that he agreed with the conclusion that the interference with the applicant's right to freedom of expression was lawful and that the domestic courts had not admitted any violation of Article 10 of the Convention in relation to the comments posted on the applicant's Facebook wall.

However, he did not accept the extension of the applicant's liability in respect of one user's comments on the basis that they had been deleted by their author the day after they were published. Under this premise, the applicant could not be blamed for not deleting a comment from a user who deleted it in less than 24 hours. On this issue, the Judge noted that criminal law had to be interpreted strictly, and that the reasoning of the majority of the Grand Chamber constituted 'an unacceptable extension of the criminal charge by an international court which constantly reiterates that it is not a court of fourth instance' (paragraph 5 of the Dissenting Opinion).

Judge Boshniak also dissented because he did not believe Mr. Sanchez could be prosecuted while the two authors of the controversial comments had already been convicted. Judges Wojtyczek and Zünd issued a joint dissenting opinion because they did not consider that the French government's interference with Mr. Sanchez's freedom of expression met the test of foreseeability.

1.3 *Zemmour v. France (No. 63539/19)*[6]

1.3.1 Brief Overview of the Facts of the Case

The case concerned incitement to discrimination and religious hatred against a group of people because of their membership of the Muslim religion. In a television programme the applicant, a controversial journalist, presented Muslims living in France as 'colonisers' and 'occupiers' in the struggle to 'Islamise' France, and stated that this situation meant that they had to 'make a choice between Islam and France'. He was convicted by French courts of 'inciting discrimination and religious hatred' against the Muslim community. The complaint was based on Article 10 of the Convention.

1.3.2 Position of the Court

As in the previous cases in this section, the Court did not find a violation of Article 10 of the Convention. It noted that the applicant's conviction was based on the characterisation of the offence as inciting discrimination and religious hatred against a group of people because of their membership of the Muslim religion (paragraph 56). Since the alleged statements were made by the applicant while he was a guest on a prime-time television programme as a prominent journalist and polemicist (paragraph 58), and their essence was that Muslims were a threat to public safety and republican values, the Court concluded that the reasons given by the domestic courts for commencing the conviction process, even though they did not expressly refer to Article 10 of the Convention, were sufficient and relevant to justify the impugned interference. The small fine that was awarded to the applicant also indicated, in the Court's opinion, that the interference was proportionate to the aim pursued (paragraph 65). Thus, there was no violation of Article 10 of the Convention.

1.3.3 Intermediate Conclusions

The European Court of Human Rights reflects a delicate balance between upholding the freedom of speech and protecting religious sensibilities from harmful and discriminatory expressions, highlighting its position on various issues including deliberate insults to religious figures, the responsibilities of politicians and broad Islamophobic statements.

In *E.S. v. Austria*, the applicant was criticised for making derogatory statements about the Prophet Muhammad, calling him a paedophile. The Court upheld the conviction, stating that freedom of speech did not extend to deliberate insults that could incite religious intolerance. The European Court of

6 Zemmour v. France—63539/19 [2022] ECHR 1130 (20 December 2022).

Human Rights emphasised that such statements were not protected under Article 10 of the European Convention on Human Rights, which guarantees freedom of expression, as they were likely to provoke justified indignation and pose a risk to religious harmony.

While the ECtHR protects religious sentiments from deliberate insults, it also upholds the principle that religious associations must tolerate the criticism and denial of their dogmas, provided that such expressions do not incite violence. This principle was reiterated in the context of various rulings in which the Court emphasised that freedom of expression includes the right to critique and deny religious beliefs. However, this tolerance has limits, especially when statements cross into hate speech or incitement to violence. The Court's jurisprudence thus delineates a clear boundary between acceptable criticism and harmful, intolerant speech.

In *Sanchez v. France*, the ECtHR addressed the issue of politicians' responsibility for Islamophobic content posted on their social media accounts. The case involved a politician who claimed he was not responsible for the Islamophobic posts made by his assistants, which he quickly deleted. The Court held that politicians are accountable for the content of their social media platforms, regardless of who posts it. It emphasised that politicians bear a heightened responsibility to prevent and address hate speech, especially due to their influential role in society. The ruling highlighted the obligation of public figures actively to manage and take responsibility for their online presence to avoid the spread of Islamophobic and discriminatory content. Despite the applicant's objections, the Court found no violation of Article 10 of the Convention.

The Court clarified its position on broad Islamophobic statements in the later case of *Zemmour v. France*. This case involved a public figure who made sweeping derogatory remarks about Muslims, suggesting that all Muslims were inherently problematic. The ECtHR ruled that such generalisations and Islamophobic statements were not protected under freedom of speech. It found that these statements amounted to hate speech, which was excluded from the protection of Article 10. The Court's approach ensures that while individuals are free to critique and debate religious beliefs, they must do so in a manner that respects the dignity and rights of religious communities, particularly in an increasingly pluralistic Europe.

2 Offences against Religious Practices

2.1 *Yilmaz v. Turkey* (*No. 36607/06*)[7]

2.1.1 Brief Overview of the Facts of the Case

The applicant was a teacher of religious culture and worked in the state education system. He successfully passed a competition that was supposed to allow him to work abroad. Subsequently, he even participated in a preparation seminar. However, the report following a security directive indicated that his wife wore a Muslim head covering outside work and that the applicant's home was divided into male and female halves. On this basis, the Ministry's evaluation commission refused to allow the applicant to work abroad. The complaint was based on Article 8 of the Convention.

Position of the Court

The Court found a violation of Article 8 of the Convention. It considered that the refusal to appoint faced by the applicant constituted an interference with his right to respect for his private life (paragraph 43). First, the Ministry of Education, citing the principle of public interest and the imperatives of the need to justify this decision, did not provide an explanation of the reasons for refusing the appointment (paragraph 45). Nor did the Commission make a decision on the applicant's skills or ability to perform the functions in question but took into account only the results of the security check (paragraph 46).

Since it remains unclear to what extent the wearing of the veil by the applicant's wife and his behaviour at home may have on the effect of undermining the requirements of the public interest or the need for educational and educational services, the Court concluded that there had been a violation of Article 8 of the Convention.

2.2 *Tagiyev and Huseynov v. Azerbaijan* (*No. 13274/08*)[8]

2.2.1 Brief Overview of the Facts of the Case

This case also concerns punishment for criticism of Islam, like *E.S. v. Austria* and *Zemmour v. France*. However, its placement in this section is that in the present case the applicants did not criticise out of Islamophobia or general hostility towards Muslims. On the contrary, the applicants, being within the Islamic tradition, were critical of certain cultural trends and practices within it. Thus, in our view, their persecution was not related to their criticism, but to the way they understood and practised Islam.

---

7 Yilmaz v. Turkey—36607/06 [2010] ECHR 117 (19 January 2010).

8 Tagiyev and Huseynov v. Azerbaijan—13274/08 [2019] ECHR 875 (5 December 2019).

Both applicants in the case were citizens of Azerbaijan. In November 2006 the first applicant wrote an article for a newspaper of which the second applicant was the editor-in-chief. This article was part of a series comparing Western and Eastern values, as well as the role of religious traditions in the formation of such values. The article, entitled 'Europe and Us', drew criticism from some Azerbaijani and Iranian religious figures and groups. A prominent Iranian religious leader issued a religious fatwa calling for the death of the applicants.

After the publication of the article, a criminal case was opened against the applicants under Article 283 of the Criminal Code of Azerbaijan, which prohibits 'incitement of religious hatred'. The District Court ordered the applicants to be detained pending trial.

A forensic linguistic and Islamic assessment of the article was also commissioned. The final report described certain comments, particularly those relating to morality in Islam, the Prophet Muhammad, Muslims living in Europe and Eastern philosophers, as inciting religious hatred and enmity.

In May 2007, on the basis of the prepared report, the domestic court found the applicants guilty and sentenced them to three and four years' imprisonment respectively. In December 2007, the applicants were released from prison following a presidential pardon after spending more than a year in prison.

The applicants complained that their conviction for the publication amounted to an unjustified interference with their right to freedom of expression under Article 10 of the European Convention on Human Rights.

In 2011, the first applicant was stabbed to death by an unknown person while returning home from work. His murder was part of a separate case.

2.2.2 Position of the Court

The Court found a violation of Article 10 of the Convention. It stated that the case involved weighing the conflicting interests of the exercise of two fundamental freedoms, namely the applicants' right to communicate to the public their views on religion in the press, on the one hand, and the rights of others to respect their freedom of thought, conscience and religion, on the other hand. The Court also reiterated that a religious group had to tolerate others' denial of its religious beliefs and even the promotion by others of doctrines hostile to their faith, provided that the statements in question do not incite hatred or religious intolerance (paragraph 44).

The Court was of the view that the article in dispute contained several remarks about Islam and its social and philosophical implications. From reading the entire text it was clear that the article was mainly concerned with a comparison between Western and Eastern values (paragraph 45) Therefore, the article should be considered not only in the context of the issue concerning religious beliefs, but also in that a discussion on an issue of public interest, namely the role of religion in society and its role in the development of society.

Since the domestic courts did not provide any explanation of why the specific remarks contained in the article constituted incitement to religious hatred and hostility and examined the alleged remarks in isolation from the general context and content of the article, without assessing the author's intention, they upset the balance between the rights protected by Articles 9 and 10 of the Convention (paragraph 47). Having regard also to the severity of the applicants' punishment, the Court concluded that the applicants' criminal convictions were disproportionate to the aims pursued and, accordingly, not 'necessary in a democratic society'. Accordingly, there had been a violation of Article 10 of the Convention.

2.3 *Sardar Babayev v. Azerbaijan (No. 34015/17 and 26896/18)*[9]

2.3.1 Brief Overview of the Facts of the Case

The present two complaints related to the pre-trial detention and subsequent criminal conviction of the applicant, a local Islamic cleric, for preaching and leading Friday prayers in a mosque. The applicant's crime was that he had carried out the activities of an Islamic cleric, having had a foreign Islamic religious education, which is prohibited by Azerbaijani law. The applicant considered that this violated Article 9 of the Convention.

2.3.2 Position of the Court

The Court found a violation of Article 9 of the Convention. Thus, in its opinion, there was no indication that the Islamic religious rites and rituals carried out by the applicant contained any expressions or constituted any incorrect actions, such as, for example, the desire to spread, incite or justify hatred, discrimination or intolerance, or otherwise undermine the ideals and values of a democratic society (paragraph 75). Thus, he was punished solely for failure to comply with new legal requirements introduced in December 2015 and applicable to citizens of the Republic of Azerbaijan who had received their religious education abroad.

In the Court's view, punishing a person simply for performing religious rites and rituals on the basis of his or her place of study can hardly be considered compatible with the exercise of freedom of religion protected by Article 9 of the Convention (paragraph 77). In addition, the Court noted that a prohibition on any person who had received a religious education abroad from practising

9 Sardar Babayev v. Azerbaijan—34015/17 [2024] ECHR 88 (1 February 2024).

Islamic religious rites and rituals might constitute an appropriate tool to combat religious extremism (paragraph 78).

In these circumstances, the Court concluded that the interference with the applicant's right to freedom of religion did not pursue any 'urgent social need'. Accordingly, there had been a violation of Article 9 of the Convention.

2.3.3 Intermediate Conclusions

The Court's jurisprudence on cases involving offences against the religious practices of Muslims underlines the principles of religious freedom, non-discrimination and the right to freedom of expression.

In *Yilmaz v. Turkey*, the ECtHR addressed the issue of workplace discrimination against a believer who followed strict Islamic practices at home. The applicant, Yilmaz, disputed that his dismissal was based on his religious practices and personal life, which were in accordance with Islamic norms but perceived as contrary to the secular values of the State. The Court held that it was impermissible to discriminate against individuals at work based on their private adherence to religious norms. The decision emphasises that one's personal religious practices should not be grounds for discrimination in employment, particularly when these practices did not interfere with one's professional responsibilities. This case reinforces the principle that secularism should not be imposed to the extent that it infringes individuals' religious freedoms in their private lives.

Tagiyev and Huseynov v. Azerbaijan illustrates the ECtHR's stance on the balance between freedom of expression and religious sensitivity. The applicants, Tagiyev and Huseynov, were imprisoned for publishing an article that criticised Islam in a polemical manner. The Court ruled that imprisoning individuals for expressing critical views about a religion constituted a violation of Article 10 of the European Convention on Human Rights, which guarantees the freedom of expression. The ECtHR emphasised that, while freedom of expression may be restricted to protect public order and religious harmony, such restrictions had to be proportionate and necessary in a democratic society. The Court noted that critical statements should be assessed in the context of the entire article, considering the intent and potential impact of the publication. This ruling emphasises the importance of protecting freedom of expression, even when it involves criticism of religious beliefs, as long as it does not incite violence or hatred.

In *Sardar Babayev v. Azerbaijan*, the ECtHR dealt with the issue of restrictions on religious activities based on the applicant's foreign religious education. Babayev, who had received a religious education abroad, was prohibited from engaging in religious activities in Azerbaijan. The Court found that this restriction violated his rights under Article 9 of the European Convention on Human Rights, which protects the freedom of thought, conscience and religion. The ECtHR held that prohibiting individual from practising their religion solely because they have received education abroad is unjustifiable and discriminatory. The ruling emphasised that States must respect the right to religious education and practice, irrespective of where the education was obtained, provided it does not contravene public safety, health or morals.

The Court consistently emphasises that while States may impose certain restrictions in order to maintain public order and secularism, these restrictions must not disproportionately infringe individuals' rights to religious freedom and expression. Discrimination based on private religious practices, unwarranted imprisonment for critical expression, and unjustified restrictions on religious activities due to a foreign education are all considered incompatible with the principles enshrined in the European Convention on Human Rights. Through its jurisprudence, the ECtHR reaffirms the importance of protecting religious diversity and ensuring that individuals can freely practise their faith without fear of discrimination or undue interference.

CHAPTER 12

Family Law

The European Court of Human Rights frequently encounters complex family law cases involving the religious freedoms of Muslims. These cases are intricate due to the intersection of Islamic law and national secular legislation, and they encompass a broad spectrum of issues, from spousal rights and obligations to inheritance, the recognition of religious marriages and child-rearing practices.[1]

In family law cases, the ECtHR must often navigate through the relationship between Islamic law and national secular legislation. One prominent issue is the recognition or non-recognition of religious marriages. Islamic marriages, which may not always be registered with state authorities, can lead to complications in legal matters such as inheritance, divorce and spousal support.

For instance, disputes may arise when spouses seek legal recognition of their marriage to claim inheritance rights or spousal benefits. National laws in many European countries require civil registration of marriages for them to be legally recognised, and this can conflict with the practices of some Muslim communities where religious ceremonies are considered sufficient. In its jurisprudence, the European Court of Human Rights generally upholds the primacy of state-registered marriage, particularly in cases where disputes arise regarding marital status, inheritance and other legal matters. However, the Court also demonstrates an awareness and respect for certain institutions of Islamic law, such as *kafala*—a system of guardianship or sponsorship for children, often used in contexts where formal adoption is not recognised or practised. While the ECtHR generally upholds the principle of state-registered marriage, its approach to cases involving *kafala* reflects a nuanced understanding of the diverse cultural and religious practices within member states.

The rights of parents and children form another critical area in which the ECtHR must reconcile Islamic practices with secular national laws. One of the most contentious issues is the removal of children from disadvantaged Muslim migrant families and the placing of them in families with a different cultural and religious background.

Child welfare cases often involve complex considerations of the best interests of the child, which may sometimes conflict with the religious practices

1 Büchler, Andrea, 'Islamic Family Law in Europe? From Dichotomies to Discourse—or: Beyond Cultural and Religious Identity in Family Law,' *International Journal of Law in Context* 8.2 (2012), pp. 196–210.

and beliefs of the parents. The ECtHR's task is to ensure that any interference with family life is justified and proportionate. This involves assessing whether the State's actions are necessary to protect the child and whether less intrusive measures could achieve the same objective.

In cases where children are placed in foster care or adopted by non-Muslim families, the Court examines whether this placement respects the child's right to maintain their religious and cultural identity. The ECtHR recognises that uprooting children from their cultural and religious environment can have profound psychological impacts. Therefore, it scrutinises the State's decisions to ensure that they are in the child's best interests and that efforts are made to place the child in an environment that respects their cultural and religious heritage.

The ECtHR's flexible approach in family law cases allows it to consider the diverse social, legal, cultural and technical contexts of the member states. This adaptability is crucial because the concept of 'family life' under Article 8 of the Convention is not rigidly defined. Instead, the Court evaluates whether the specific circumstances of a complaint fall within the scope of rights protected by Article 8.

1 Rights of Spouses

1.1 *Janis Khan v. United Kingdom (No. 11579/85)*[2]

1.1.1 Brief Overview of the Facts of the Case

The applicant, a Muslim of British nationality, removed a girl aged 14½ years from her home and married her, according to Islamic religious rites, against the wishes of her parents. A little over a year later, the girl's father managed to take her home by force. The applicant was convicted of kidnapping and sexual contact with a minor. The applicant alleged a violation of Articles 9 and 12 of the Convention.

Article 12 of the European Convention on Human Rights—Right to marry

Men and women of marriageable age have the right to marry and to found a family, according to the national laws governing the exercise of this right.

2 Janis Khan v. United Kingdom, No. 11579/85 (1986) 48 DR 253 (7 July 1986).

1.1.2 Position of the Court

The Court declared the complaint inadmissible. According to the British law in force at that time, marriage for a girl was possible only from the age of 18 and, in exceptional cases, with the consent of the parents, from 16. Sexual relations with a minor under 16 years of age was a separate criminal offence. The Court noted that Article 12 of the Convention applies only to persons who have reached marriageable age in terms of national law. Therefore, marriage to a person of lesser age was illegal and could not be protected by the Convention. It followed that there was no violation of the Articles in question.

1.2 *Serife Yiğit v. Turkey (No. 3976/05)*[3]

1.2.1 Brief Overview of the Facts of the Case

The applicant was in a religious Islamic marriage in which she had had several children. After the death of her husband, the applicant applied to government authorities to recognise her marriage and enter information about her youngest daughter into the civil registry. The district court granted the second motion but denied the motion to recognise the marriage. The applicant also applied to the pension fund to transfer her late husband's old-age pension and health insurance to her and her daughter. Benefits were provided only to the daughter and not to her mother, on the ground that the marriage had not been legally recognised. The applicant appealed this decision unsuccessfully. Relying on Article 8 of the Convention (right to respect for family life), the applicant complained about the refusal of the Turkish courts to transfer to her the social security rights of her deceased partner.

1.2.2 Position of the Court

The Court did not find any violations of Article 8 of the Convention. It noted that the applicant, together with her partner, had decided to live in a religious marriage and start a family. She and her late husband were able to live a peaceful family life, without any interference from the national authorities. Thus, the fact that they chose a religious form of marriage and did not enter into a civil marriage did not entail any penalties—either administrative or criminal—such as preventing the applicant from leading an effective family life for the purposes of Article 8 (paragraph 101). Thus, the Court did not see any signs of state interference in the applicant's family life.

And since Article 8 of the Convention does not impose an obligation on the State to recognise a religious marriage, the fact that the applicant does not have

3 Serife Yiğit v. Turkey—3976/05 [2010] ECHR 1672 (2 November 2010).

the status of an heir under the provisions of the Civil Code governing inheritance and domestic social security legislation does not mean that there has been a violation of her rights under Article 8.

Judge Rozakis, supporting the opinion, noted that he believed the real comparison should have been between long-standing cohabitation and marriage as understood by domestic law. Given the special status of marital relationships, States had leeway in treating them differently in matters like taxation and social security. Thus, in this case, the absence of social security benefits did not violate the Convention. However, as societal norms evolve, perhaps the Court should reconsider its stance on the distinction between marriage and other forms of family life regarding social security benefits.

Judge Kovler raised some objections to this decision. He disagreed with the Court's assessment of Islamic marriage law. In his opinion, portraying it in a reductive manner and overlooking women's rights within it were problematic. A deeper analysis of the financial aspects of Islamic marriage would have provided a more nuanced understanding. Additionally, the Court's judgment on Islamic values demonstrated cultural activism, which was concerning.

Considering other human rights instruments like the Universal Islamic Declaration of Human Rights could have prevented hasty conclusions. Judge Kovler urged the European Court of Human Rights to adopt a more anthropological approach, exploring differences with sensitivity. Otherwise, it would risk perpetuating Eurocentric attitudes.

1.3 *Molla Sali v. Greece (No. 20452/14)*[4]

1.3.1 Brief Overview of the Facts of the Case

The applicant was the widow of a Greek citizen from the Muslim minority who, in his formal will, left all his property to her. However, in inheritance proceedings in a dispute with the deceased's sisters, the Greek courts considered that the will had no effect and applied the Muslim religious law of inheritance, which in Greece applied specifically to Greeks of the Muslim faith.

Because of this, the applicant was deprived of three quarters of the inheritance in favour of the deceased's sisters, whom the court of first instance had recognised as co-owners of his property. Having failed to challenge this decision in Greece, the applicant lodged a complaint with the ECtHR on the basis of a violation of Articles 6 and 14 of the Convention (prohibition of discrimination), read in conjunction with Article 1 of Protocol No. 1 to the Convention.

4 Molla Sali v. Greece—20452/14 [2018] ECHR 1048 (19 December 2018).

1.3.2 Position of the Court

The Court found a violation, deferring the issue of compensation to a later date. Initially, it is important to highlight that the Court focused solely on Article 14 in conjunction with Article 1 of Protocol No. 1, excluding Article 6(1) of the Convention. The examination unfolded in three main stages. First, the Court assessed whether the disputed elements qualified as 'possession' under Article 1 of Protocol No. 1, which indeed they did (paragraph 124–126). Second, it compared the applicant's situation with that of a beneficiary under a civil law will, finding differential treatment based on religion. However, the Court stressed that differential treatment must be objectively and reasonably justified (paragraphs 135–137). The Government discussed that applying Islamic law was justified by international agreements and the nature of the property (paragraph 146). Yet, the Court found this justification lacking.

The Court noted the legal uncertainty stemming from divergent case law on the application of Islamic law in Thrace, which conflicted moreover with the rule of law. It was emphasised that freedom of religion did not require a special regime granting particular privileges to religious communities, and denying access to regular law violated the right to self-identification. Consequently, the Courtly unanimously concluded a violation of Article 14 of the Convention in conjunction with Article 1 of Protocol No. 1 (paragraphs 155–156).

In his concurring opinion, Judge Mits agreed with the outcome but raised concerns about addressing the complaint based on the applicant's sex and the implementation of a special religious regime in a culturally diverse context. He ultimately concluded that there had been a violation of the aforementioned Articles based on both the applicant's and her husband's religion.

1.3.3 Intermediate Conclusions

One notable case that illustrates the ECtHR's stance on religious marriages is *Janis Khan v. United Kingdom*. In this case, the Court examined the legality of a religious marriage entered into before one of the spouses had reached the legal age for marriage. The Court ruled that such a marriage and subsequent cohabitation were illegal and could not be equated with a registered marriage under state law. This decision highlights the ECtHR's commitment to upholding the legal standards of marriageable age and ensuring that religious practices do not contravene these protections.

The ECtHR's decision emphasises the importance of adhering to state laws regarding the age of marriage which are designed to protect the welfare of minors. By refusing to recognise a religious marriage that violated these standards, the Court reinforced the principle that religious freedoms must be exercised within the bounds of national laws, particularly those that safeguard vulnerable individuals.

Another significant case is *Serife Yiğit v. Turkey*, where the ECtHR ruled that an ordinary religious Muslim marriage could not be equated to a state-registered marriage, regardless of its duration or the presence of children. This ruling illustrates the distinction between religious and civil marriages and the necessity for legal recognition through state registration.

The Court's decision in this case reinforces the notion that religious marriages, while culturally significant, must conform to state regulations to be recognised legally. This ensures clarity in matters of legal rights, obligations and protections for all parties involved, particularly in areas such as inheritance, spousal support and child custody.

The application of Sharia norms in secular jurisdictions, particularly those concerning inheritance, was addressed in *Molla Sali v. Greece*. The case involved the inheritance rights of a spouse under a will that was contested on the basis of Sharia law. The ECtHR ruled that applying Sharia norms in the presence of a legal will was harmful in a secular jurisdiction. Moreover, the question in *Molla Sali v. Greece* was whether the State was authorised to apply religious norms in relation to a specific group of the population professing that faith. The Court decided that secular law had to take precedence and that the imposition by the State of religious norms on individuals from a particular religious group violated the principle of equal treatment under the law. The Court added that although the application of Sharia law was based, *inter alia*, on international law, and in particular on the combined effect of Articles 42 and 45 of the Treaty of Lausanne, that should not result in the Islamic law of succession being applied in such a way as to curtail the civil rights of Greek Muslims. The aim of the treaty had not been to deprive the members of that minority of such rights, but to strengthen their protection.

By asserting that secular law takes precedence in such cases, the ECtHR protects individuals' rights dispose of their property freely through a legal will, without being overridden by religious norms. This ensures that legal processes remain consistent and predictable, providing certainty and protection to all parties involved.

In each of these cases the ECtHR underscored the importance of legal recognition and protection under state laws, while also acknowledging the significance of religious practices. In doing so, the Court maintains a balance that respects religious diversity while ensuring that legal standards and protections are uniformly applied.

2 Rights of Parents and Children. The Right to Be Raised in Islamic Culture

2.1 *Harroudj v. France (No. 43631/09)*[5]

2.1.1 Brief Overview of the Facts of the Case

The case concerns the increasingly widespread Islamic legal institution in Europe—*kafala*. Adoption is considered incompatible with Sharia law. However, the use of *kafala* is permitted—a form of guardianship over a child without recognition of a family relationship with him.

Kafala is deeply connected with upbringing in the Islamic tradition due to its emphasis on the protection, education and care of a child, much as how parents would care for their own offspring. In the context of kafala, an adult (the *kafil*) takes on the responsibility of providing for, raising and protecting a child (*makfoul*), ensuring their welfare and development.[6] This aligns closely with the Islamic values of ensuring the wellbeing of children, providing for their education, and fostering a supportive and caring environment for their growth.

However, kafala differs from adoption in a crucial way. In the Islamic tradition, kafala is a form of guardianship rather than a redefinition of family ties. It does not equate to the legal or social transformation of the child into the adoptive parent's family line. The child remains recognised as belonging to their biological family, which prevents the falsification of bloodlines—a concept considered critical in Islam. The Islamic perspective of family lineage is a significant factor in distinguishing kafala from adoption, reinforcing the notion that while children under kafala receive care and education, their biological identity remains intact. Therefore, kafala can be seen as an institution in Islamic tradition that illustrates the importance of nurturing children within the boundaries of established family and societal norms, without altering their fundamental identity or bloodlines.

In this case, the applicant—a young French woman—took an Algerian child under her *kafala*. A few years later, she petitioned the French authorities for a full adoption at the Lyon High Court on the grounds that it was in the best interests of the child. The court recognised that, in accordance with the provisions of the Civil Code, the adoption of a child whose local law of the country of nationality prohibits adoption could not be permitted. Islamic law does not

5 Harroudj v. France—43631/09 (4 October 2012).

6 Büchler, A., and Schneider Kayasseh, E., 'Fostering and Adoption in Islamic Law—Under Consideration of the Laws of Morocco, Egypt, and the United Arab Emirates,' *Electronic Journal of Islamic and Middle Eastern Law* (EJIMEL), 6, 2018, pp. 31–39.

allow adoption, which *de jure* results in the creation of family ties comparable to biological descent. The applicant was unable to appeal this decision.

She lodged an application with the ECtHR, citing Article 8 on respect for private life and Article 14 on discrimination, emphasising that the law resulted in discrimination against the child in her care.

2.1.2 Position of the Court

The Court did not find a violation of Article 8 of the Convention. Referring to various international treaties recognising kafala, it noted that the applicant's refusal was mainly due to the French authorities' desire to respect the spirit and purpose of international conventions (paragraph 50). The Court considered that the recognition of kafala by international law was a decisive factor in assessing how States addressed the issue in their national laws and provided for any choice of law issues that might arise.

The Court also noted that, under the current legal regime between the applicant and the child, the applicant exercised parental rights giving her the right to make any decision in the interests of the child (paragraph 51). However, there were ways to circumvent the restrictions associated with the inability to adopt a child (for example, it is possible to draw up a will allowing the child to inherit the applicant's property, or to appoint a legal guardian in the event of the death of the adoptive parent). According to the Court, there were compelling reasons for the legislation prohibiting the adoption of children under kafala (for example, it excludes the possibility for such a child to obtain French citizenship within a shortened period of time, which facilitated the integration of children of foreign origin into France without immediately cutting them off from the rules of the country of their origin, respects cultural pluralism and strikes a fair balance between the public interest and the interests of the applicant).

For the above reasons, the Court held that, having regard to the State's margin of appreciation in such matters, there was no violation of the applicant's right to respect for her family life. Accordingly, there was no violation of Article 8 of the Convention.

2.2 *Kilic v. Austria (No. 27700/15)*[7]

2.2.1 Brief Overview of the Facts of the Case

The applicants were a married couple of Turkish origin and Muslim faith. They had five children, born in 1999, 2000, 2004, 2007 and 2010 respectively. As early

7 Kilic v. Austria—27700/15 [2023] ECHR 10 (12 January 2023).

as in 2006, the applicants' three eldest children were found alone on the street in an alarming state of neglect. Shortly afterwards, the children were found left alone in the family's apartment, which was in an alarming sanitary condition.

As a result, the Vienna Youth Office (*Jugendwohlfahrtsträger*—hereinafter 'YWO') placed the three children in an orphanage as an emergency measure, temporarily removing them from their family. Since the applicants subsequently cooperated with YWO and renovated their apartment, the children were again placed in their care. In October 2010, information again appeared that the applicants' apartment was in an alarming sanitary and hygienic condition.

After this, all the children were again taken away from the applicants. The three older ones were again placed in an orphanage; the two younger ones were placed in foster families of Austrian Christians who did not speak Turkish. According to the applicants, this deprived them of their Turkish and Muslim identity, alienating them from their culture and religion. Accordingly, Articles 8 and 9 of the Convention had been violated.

2.2.2 Position of the Court

The Court rejected the applicants' complaint. It declared unfounded the applicants' arguments that the initial placement of the three older children in an orphanage, with the restriction of their visitation rights and the refusal of their relatives' applications for guardianship, was excessive (paragraph 104). It also noted that there were very few Turkish and/or Muslim adoptive families in the Vienna area, despite active efforts by the authorities to encourage more such families to apply (paragraph 100). Therefore, both younger children were placed in foster families that were particularly open to other cultures and religions. In addition, according to the Government's undisputed submissions, the YWO noted that the adoptive parents spoke to the children about their cultural roots and encouraged their interest in them (paragraph 140). However, the Court noted that the applicants did not express a specific desire to have a specific foster family at the time of placement of the children (paragraph 148) and openly opposed the transfer of the children to relatives. Moreover, when the applicants first raised their objections to the foster families of their younger children, one of them had already lived with his foster mother for at least one and a half years, and the other with his foster parents for several months (paragraph 150).

Despite the applicants' claims that the cross decoration on the arm of one of their children was a substitute for his cultural identity, the Court did not establish any deliberate policy of de-Islamising or otherwise culturally indoctrinating removed children (paragraph 152). At the same time, the Court condemned the applicants' attempt to abduct their daughter from her foster family on those grounds (paragraph 154) and justified the suspension of the applicants' right to visit the children following this incident (paragraph 155).

Having regard to the measures taken by the guardianship authorities to teach the removed children the Turkish language and culture (paragraphs 158–160), the Court held that the authorities had given due regard to the applicants' interest in having their children brought up in accordance with their cultural, religious and linguistic background. Accordingly, there had been no violation of Article 8 of the Convention, interpreted separately and in the light of Article 9.

Judge Huseynov delivered a dissenting opinion. There had been a violation of Article 8 of the Convention. He claimed that the Austrian authorities had failed to fulfil their obligations to preserve the cultural and linguistic identity of children in foster care. Judge Huseynov notes that contact between parents and children was extremely limited, which did not take into account the importance of maintaining contact with the religious and cultural environment. It also highlights restrictions on visiting rights and the need to take measures to preserve language links. Judge Huseynov believed that the Austrian authorities had not done enough to prevent the linguistic and cultural alienation of the children. He argued that the limited visitation and the lack of active measures to preserve the mother tongue and culture resulted in a violation of the State's positive obligations under Article 8 of the Convention.

2.3 *Abdi Ibrahim v. Norway (No. 15379/16)*[8]

2.3.1 Brief Overview of the Facts of the Case

The applicant was a Somalian national and a Muslim who arrived in Norway in 2009. In 2010 her child, A, was taken into public care. In 2014 the Child Care Protective Authorities decided to deprive the applicant of parental responsibility for A and approved the adoption of A by a Christian family. The decision was upheld by a final Supreme Court decision in 2015.

The applicant complains under Article 8 of the Convention that her right to respect for her family life had been infringed by the domestic authorities' decision to deprive her of the custody of A and to allow A's adoption.

Furthermore, the applicant complained under Article 9 of the Convention that the Norwegian courts had approved A's adoption by foster parents of the Christian faith who would baptise him and give him a Christian name.

8 Abdi Ibrahim v. Norway—15379/16 [2020] ECHR 334 (12 May 2020).

2.3.2 Position of the Court

The Court found a violation of Article 8 of the Convention. It noted that the adoption of an applicant's child by a foster family against her will as a biological mother was an extremely complex matter and required a very careful approach (paragraph 148). Assessing the case materials, it concluded that the domestic authorities had not attempted to strike a genuine balance between the interests of the child and those of his biological family, but had focused solely on interests, and had not seriously considered any possibility of maintaining contact between the child and his biological family (paragraph 151).

In this context, the Court was not convinced that the competent domestic authorities had given due regard to the potential significance of the fact that the applicant had not applied to have the guardianship order set aside but had simply objected to the adoption on the ground that she wished to retain the right to communicate with her child (paragraph 43). In this regard, given that the High Court's decision was largely based on an assessment of X's attachment to his stepfamily, the factual basis on which it relied in making that assessment appeared to reveal flaws in the decision-making process.

Moreover, the Court noted that the reasons set out in the domestic courts' decision focused essentially on the potential consequences of removing the child from his adoptive parents and returning him to the applicant, rather than on grounds for ceasing all contact between the biological mother and the child. For example, the domestic courts appeared to place greater weight on the adoptive parents' opposition to an 'open adoption' than on the applicant's interest in continuing her family life with her child through contact (paragraph 153).

As regards the impossibility of raising the applicant's child in Islamic traditions, the Court stated that the applicant's rights under Article 8 of the Convention, as interpreted in the light of Article 9, could be respected not only by finding an adoptive family appropriate to her cultural and religious background (paragraph 161). Although the authorities sought to find a suitable family for the applicant's child, they did not take into account the possibility of preserving cultural ties with Islam by allowing the applicant to see her child.

The Court was therefore not satisfied that, by depriving the applicant of her parental responsibility in relation to her child and allowing his adoption by foster parents, the domestic authorities had not given sufficient weight to the applicant's right. The Court was also of the view that the decision-making process leading to the eventual termination of the applicant's relationship with the child was not conducted in a manner that ensured that all her views and interests were given due consideration. Accordingly, there has been a violation of Article 8.

All the Judges expressed support for the decision. Dissenting opinions were expressed only regarding the calculation of compensation.

2.3.3 Intermediate Conclusions

The European Court of Human Rights has addressed these cases concerning the rights of parents and children, particularly focusing on the right to be raised in an Islamic cultural context. This issue is complex, as it involves balancing the protection of religious freedoms with the principles of state law and the best interests of the child. The following discussion explores significant cases in which the ECtHR has established key precedents on these matters.

In *Harroudj v. France*, a French woman sought to adopt a child she had taken from Algeria under the Islamic form of guardianship known as kafala. However, the French authorities refused to recognise this guardianship as equivalent to adoption under French law. The Court emphasised that such a refusal ensured legal clarity and protection for the child. While *kafala* is recognised by international law, it does not confer the same legal rights and obligations as full adoption under French law. Therefore, the State's decision to uphold its adoption laws did not violate the woman's rights.

The ECtHR reasoned that while kafala establishes a form of guardianship, it does not confer the same legal rights and obligations as full adoption. By not recognising kafala as equivalent to adoption, the State ensures that children have secure and legally recognised parental relationships. This ruling stresses the importance that the Court places on the legal clarity and protection provided by state-recognised adoption processes, even when it conflicts with religious practices.

In *Kilic v. Austria*, the ECtHR examined the issue of placing children from Muslim families into foster care environments that do not match their ethnic and cultural background. The case involved children from a dysfunctional Muslim family who were placed by juvenile justice services into a non-Muslim foster family due to the unavailability of a Muslim one. The Court found this placement to be in accordance with the European Convention on Human Rights, emphasising the necessity of ensuring the children's safety and well-being above maintaining their cultural and religious background.

The ECtHR acknowledged that while cultural and religious continuity is important, the primary concern must be the child's best interests. The Court reasoned that in situations where a suitable foster family of the same cultural and religious background was not available, it was permissible to place the child in a different environment to ensure their safety and welfare. This decision highlights the Court's pragmatic approach to prioritising the immediate needs and protection of the child over cultural considerations.

Abdi Ibrahim v. Norway further illustrates the ECtHR's approach to balancing the rights of biological parents with the State's duty to protect children. In this case, a Muslim mother was completely deprived of her right to see her child, who was placed in a foster family with different traditions. The mother's objections and her wish to have her child raised within an Islamic cultural context were not adequately considered by the state authorities.

The ECtHR ruled that this complete deprivation of the mother's right to see her child and the failure to consider her wishes regarding the child's cultural upbringing were not justified. The court emphasised that the State must take into account the biological parent's opinion and cultural background when making decisions about the child's placement, provided that doing so did not jeopardise the child's welfare.

This ruling illustrates the importance of respecting the biological rights of parents and their cultural and religious wishes within the framework of the child's best interests. The Court highlighted the need for a balanced approach that considered both the protection of the child and the preservation of their cultural and familial ties.

These decisions reflect the ECtHR's overarching principle that while religious freedoms are protected, they must be exercised within the framework of state laws designed to protect the welfare and rights of children. This balanced approach ensures that children's immediate needs are met, while also respecting the cultural and religious values of their families as much as possible within the bounds of the law.

Conclusion

In our book we explore the intricate and often controversial realm of how the European Court of Human Rights handles cases concerning Islam and Muslim individuals. Our detailed analysis covers the Court's jurisprudence, identifying key themes and landmark cases that exemplify how the ECtHR navigates the balance between religious freedoms and state interests.

Throughout this book, we have reviewed approximately 70 cases. Our selection criteria were based on the frequency with which these cases were cited in ECtHR practice, as well as their relevance to the topics addressed in each of the 12 chapters. The classification of these cases is not rigid and is provisional, as multiple legal issues can be present in a single case.

We begin by emphasising the ECtHR's foundational commitment to safeguarding religious freedom, as outlined in Article 9 of the European Convention on Human Rights. However, the Court frequently faces the challenging task of weighing individual rights against broader national interests like public order, safety and secularism. This challenge is particularly evident in prominent cases such as *Leyla Şahin v. Turkey*, where the Court upheld a ban on headscarves in universities to uphold secular principles and public order, and *S.A.S. v. France*, where it supported France's ban on face coverings, citing the need for social cohesion and protecting others' rights.

A central theme in our analysis is the ECtHR's application of the margin of appreciation doctrine. This principle grants States a certain degree of flexibility in balancing individual rights with public interests, acknowledging that national authorities are often better equipped to assess local needs. The margin of appreciation results in varying levels of protection for religious freedoms across different countries, reflecting diverse cultural and societal contexts. We note that this doctrine is often used in cases involving Islam, where national secular policies frequently clash with individual religious practices.

We also highlight the complexity of the legal issues in many of these cases. A single case can give rise to multiple legal questions, making classification challenging. For example, cases may involve issues of religious expression, non-discrimination and the interaction between religion and public policies. This complexity forces the Court to navigate a web of interconnected legal principles and societal concerns, adding layers of difficulty to its decisions.

A particularly intriguing aspect of these cases is their potential to disrupt established normative legal categories under the ECtHR, sparking new forms of political thought and prompting a re-evaluation of both historical and theoretical foundations of modern liberal political orders. These controversies introduce two critical questions for ECtHR jurisprudence: the appropriate scope of the right to religious freedom and the conceptual relationship between religion and the public sphere, not just within European nation states but also within the supranational framework of the Strasbourg Court.

Our book does not avoid discussing the criticisms and controversies surrounding the ECtHR's handling of cases involving Muslims. Some argue that the Court's deference to national authorities undermines the universality of human rights, leading to inconsistent protection across member states. Others believe that the ECtHR sometimes fails fully to understand the importance of certain religious practices for Muslims, resulting in decisions that inadequately protect their rights. Conversely, the Court is also criticised for perceived overreach and for imposing external standards on domestic legal systems, highlighting the tension between universal human rights and national sovereignty.

We emphasise the importance of the ECtHR's ongoing dialogue with national courts and its evolving interpretation of the Convention. The Court's dynamic approach allows it to adapt to changing societal values and norms while maintaining the core principles of human rights. This interpretive flexibility is essential for addressing the diverse and complex issues related to the religious freedoms of Muslims in Europe. The ECtHR's jurisprudence on Islam is not static; it evolves in response to new cases and broader societal changes, reflecting the dynamic nature of European societies.

We argue that the complex historical and normative relationship between Christianity and secularism continues to shape the modern public sphere and the right to religious liberty. Claims of rights by Muslims have highlighted both the historical contingency and cultural specificity of these norms and legal structures. Our argument views the Court's reasoning under Article 9 as entangled with two rival liberal traditions: one that defines religious liberty in terms of value pluralism and social peace, and another that defines it more narrowly in terms of autonomy and a particular theory of justice.

In summary, our book provides a comprehensive analysis of the ECtHR's handling of cases involving Islam and religious freedoms. We highlight the Court's efforts to protect fundamental rights while balancing national interests, the complexity of legal issues and the evolving nature of its jurisprudence. By examining key cases and themes, we underscore the pivotal role of the ECtHR in shaping the landscape of religious freedom in Europe. The Court's decisions, though sometimes controversial, contribute to the broader goals of justice and human dignity, reinforcing the principles of democracy, pluralism and tolerance that underpin the European human rights system. As Europe continues to diversify, the ECtHR's role in protecting religious freedoms and fostering understanding among different cultural and religious communities remains vital.

Bibliography

Ali, Muhammad, Liu Yi Deng Liu, and Khalid, Muhammad Khabeer, 'Legality of Blasphemy in Islam: A Brief Comparison of Legislations around the World.' *Islamic Quarterly* 66.1 (2022), pp. 91–130.

An-Naim, Abdullahi Ahmed, *Islam and the Secular State: Negotiating the Future of Sharia.* (Cambridge, MA: Harvard University Press, 2008).

Aydın-Düzgit, Senem, and Tocci, Nathalie, *Turkey and the European Union.* (London and New York: Palgrave Macmillan, 2015).

Baderin, Mashood, 'Islamic Law and the Implementation of Human Rights Law: A Case Study of the International Covenant on Civil and Political Rights.' in Baderin, Mashood, and Ssenyonjo, Manisuli, eds., *International Human Rights Law: Six Decades after the UDHR and Beyond.* (Aldershot: Ashgate, 2010), pp. 337–357.

Bates, Ed, *The Evolution of the European Convention on Human Rights: From Its Inception to the Creation of a Permanent Court of Human Rights.* (Oxford: Oxford University Press, 2010).

Bleich, Erik, 'Defining and Researching Islamophobia.' *Review of Middle East Studies* 46.2 (2012), pp. 180–189.

Bravo López, Fernando, 'Towards a Definition of Islamophobia: Approximations of the Early Twentieth Century.' *Ethnic and Racial Studies* 34.4 (2011), pp. 556–573.

Büchler, Andrea, 'Islamic Family Law in Europe? From Dichotomies to Discourse—or: Beyond Cultural and Religious Identity in Family Law.' *International Journal of Law in Context* 8.2 (2012), pp. 196–210.

Büchler, Andrea, and Schneider Kayasseh, E., 'Fostering and Adoption in Islamic Law—Under Consideration of the Laws of Morocco, Egypt, and the United Arab Emirates.' *Electronic Journal of Islamic and Middle Eastern Law (EJIMEL)* 6 (2018), pp. 31–39.

Cavalcanti, Maria, 'Islamic Family Law and Legal Pluralism Approach: Case Studies of Reasonable Accommodation in Europe.' *Ius Comparatum* (2022).2, pp. 352–388.

Cesari, Jocelyne, 'Securitization of Islam in Europe: The Embodiment of Islam as an Exception.' in Jocelyne Cesari, ed., *Why the West Fears Islam: An Exploration of Muslims in Liberal Democracies* (New York: Palgrave Macmillan, 2013), pp. 83 = 105

Cambour, Marie-Bénédicte, 'The Migrant Case Law of the European Court of Human Rights: Critique and Way Forward' in Başak Çalı, Ledi Bianku, and Motoc, Iulia, eds., *Migration and the European Convention on Human Rights* (Oxford: Oxford University Press, 2021), pp. 19–43.

Di Stasio, Valentina, et al., 'Muslim by Default or Religious Discrimination? Results from a Cross-National Field Experiment on Hiring Discrimination.' *Journal of Ethnic and Migration Studies* 47.6 (2021), pp. 1305–1326.

Durham, W. Cole, ed., *Islam, Europe and Emerging Legal Issues.* (Farnham: Ashgate Publishing, 2012).

Emon, Anver M., *Religious Pluralism and Islamic Law: Dhimmis and Others in the Empire of Law*. (Oxford: Oxford University Press, 2012).

European Court of Human Rights, 'Your Application to the ECHR: How to Apply and How Your Application Is Processed.' Council of Europe, Strasbourg, France. www.echr.coe.int/documents/d/echr/your_application_eng.

European Human Rights Advocacy Centre (EHRAC), 'Kasymakhunov and Saybatalov v. Russia', European Human Rights Advocacy Centre. https://ehrac.org.uk/ru/key-ehrac-cases/kasymakhunov-saybatalov-v-russia/.

European Parliament. Resolution on the Right to Freedom of Expression and Respect for Religious Beliefs, Resolution 1510 (2006). Parliamentary Assembly, 28 June 2006. https://assembly.coe.int/nw/xml/XRef/Xref-XML2HTML-en.asp?fileid=17457.

Evans, Carolyn, 'The Islamic Scarf in the European Court of Human Rights.' *Melbourne Journal of International Law* 7 (2006), p. 52.

Fokas, Effie, 'Islam at the European Court of Human Rights.' *NAVEIÑ REET: Nordic Journal of Law and Social Research* (2021), pp. 121–144.

Freedom of Religion or Belief and Security, *Policy Guidance*. OSCE/ODIHR (2019), pp. 37–39.

Guide on Article 9 of the European Convention on Human Rights—Freedom of Thought, Conscience and Religion, updated on 31 August 2024. Council of Europe/European Court of Human Rights, 2024.

Guidelines for Educators on Countering Intolerance and Discrimination against Muslims: Addressing Islamophobia through Education (2011): 18.

Habermas, Jürgen, *The Public Sphere: An Inquiry into a Category of Bourgeois Society*. (Cambridge: Polity Press, 1989).

Halevi, Leor, *Muhammad's Grave: Death Rites and the Making of Islamic Society*. (New York: Columbia University Press, 2011).

Helbling, Marc, and Traunmüller, Richard, 'What is Islamophobia? Disentangling Citizens' Feelings toward Ethnicity, Religion and Religiosity using a Survey Experiment.' *British Journal of Political Science* 50.3 (2020), pp. 811–828.

Himeur, Chihab Mohammed, *Islam et Libertés Religieuses: Le Combat des Valeurs?* Préface by Bertrand Mathieu (Brussels: Bruylant, 2022).

Joppke, Christian, and Torpey, John, *Legal Integration of Islam: A Transatlantic Comparison*. (Cambridge MA: Harvard University Press, 2013).

Kuran, Timur, 'The Absence of the Corporation in Islamic Law: Origins and Persistence.' *The American Journal of Comparative Law* 53.4 (2005), pp. 785–834.

Mahmood, Saba, *Religious Difference in a Secular Age: A Minority Report*. (Princeton: Princeton University Press, 2015).

Martínez-Torrón, Javier, 'Islam in Strasbourg: Can Politics Substitute for Law?' in W. Cole Durham, ed., *Islam, Europe and Emerging Legal Issues* (Farnham: Ashgate, 2012), pp. 19–24.

McCrea, Ronan, 'The Ban on the Veil and European Law.' *Human Rights Law Review* 13.1 (March 2013), pp. 57–97.

Mjöll Arnardóttir, Oddný, 'Vulnerability under Article 14 of the European Convention on Human Rights: Innovation or Business as Usual?' *Oslo Law Review* 4.3 (2017), pp. 150–171.

Moniz, Jorge Botelho, 'Secularization in Europe: Causes, Consequences, and Cultural Diversity.' *Religions* 14.3 (2023), p. 423.

Müller, Reto, and Greuter, Stéphanie, *Anti-Terrorist Operations and the Right to Life—The EuropeBean Court of Human Rights Case Law from Gibraltar to Beslan.* (Bern: Editions Weblaw, 2022), p. 4.

Marshall, Paul, 'Exporting Blasphemy Restrictions: The Organisation of the Islamic Conference and the United Nations.' *The Review of Faith & International Affairs* 9.2 (2011), pp. 57–63.

Nussberger, Angelika, 'Terrorizm i Prava Cheloveka: O Pravoprimenitel'noy Praktike Evropeyskogo Suda po Pravam Cheloveka.' *Mezhdunarodnoe Pravosudie* 1 (2018), pp. 67–78.

Nanwani, Shaira, 'The Burqa Ban: An Unreasonable Limitation on Religious Freedom or a Justifiable Restriction?' *Emory International Law Review* 25 (2011), p. 1431.

Overview of the ECtHR's Case-Law on Freedom of Religion, 2013, https://kronadaran.am/wp-content/uploads/2015/02/Overview-of-the-ECtHR-Case-Law-on-Freedom-of-Religion.pdf.

Protocol No. 4 and Immigration Summary Returns of Migrants and/or Asylum-Seekers ('Push-backs'). European Court of Human Rights, Strasbourg. 1 January 2024.

Shevelev, Arseny, and Shevelev, Gyorgy, 'The Nature of the Right in a Dead Body Revisited: A Study in Comparative Legal Ideas.' *Louisiana Law Review* 83.4 (2023), p. 9.

Sikuta, Jan, 'Threats of Terrorism and the European Court of Human Rights.' *European Journal of Migration and Law* 10.1 (2008), pp. 1–10.

Sofos, Spyros A., and Tsagarousianou, Roza, *Islam in Europe: Public Spaces and Civic Networks.* (London: Palgrave Macmillan, 2013).

Tavkhelidze, Tatia, 'Islam and Secularism within the Legal Framework of the European Union.' *Journal of the Contemporary Study of Islam* 4.1 (2024), pp. 5–16.

Understanding Anti-Muslim Hate Crimes: Addressing the Security Needs of Muslim Communities: A Practical Guide (Warsaw: OSCE Office for Democratic Institutions and Human Rights, 2020).

Widelitz, Kiley, 'A Global Blasphemy Law: Protecting Believers at the Expense of Free Speech.' *Pepperdine Policy Review* Vol. 6, Article 2 (2013).

Zuriet, Jade, and Lyausheva, Svetlana, 'Muslim Identity in the Conceptual Field of Modern Religious Studies.' *SHS Web of Conferences*, vol. 72, 2019, p. 2008. https://doi.org/10.1051/shsconf/20197202008.

Zvi, Muhammad, 'Secularism and Islamic Law: Challenges in Muslim-Christian Relations.' *International Review of the Red Cross* 89.885 (2007), pp. 907–920.

Index

www.ingramcontent.com/pod-product-compliance
Lightning Source LLC
Chambersburg PA
CBHW071340230926
51846CB00002B/402
9789004745551